Silence Is Not an Option

A Memoir of Overcoming Abuse, Anxiety, and Depression

by
Argentina Parra

D1431853

First Printing: 2018

This book was edited, designed, laid out, proofread, and publicized by an Editwright team. Visit editwright.com for more Editwright works.

Developmental editing, copy editing, and book design by Andrew Doty
Cover design by Andrea Melania Rodriguez Moon
Cover photo model: Carly Angela Mazur
Proofreading by Karen L. Tucker
Published by Not Broken LLC

The author shares her experiences in encouragement and empowerment as a public speaker for classes, workshops, and special events. To contact the author, use the contact form at ArgentinaParra.com.

ISBN: 978-1-7328289-0-2

Library of Congress Control Number: 2018965008

BISAC Codes:
BIO002030 BIOGRAPHY & AUTOBIOGRAPHY / Cultural, Ethnic & Regional /
    Hispanic & Latino
BIO026000 BIOGRAPHY & AUTOBIOGRAPHY / Personal Memoirs
BIO022000 BIOGRAPHY & AUTOBIOGRAPHY / Women

The events are portrayed in this book are to the best of the author's memory. While all the stories in this book are true, some names and identifying details have been changed to protect the privacy of the people involved.

*This book is dedicated to my mother and grandmother
for always taking the time to listen to my problems and struggles
despite having many of their own.*

TABLE OF CONTENTS

INTRODUCTION

The cycle of abuse is hard to break. My mother was abused by my father nearly every day. As I grew up, I saw that behavior so often that it became a normal experience for me. Because of that, I confused love with anger and rage. I thought that those emotions were a package deal. Then I saw the movie *The Color Purple.* Oprah Winfrey played Sofia, a very strong woman who refused to be abused any longer, and her character inspired me.

For me, the movie was a wake-up call. At the time, I was married to an abusive man, but I didn't realize it. Looking back, I think I was like a lot of women in my situation. After a lifetime of dealing with bullies who supposedly loved me, I learned that the only way to live with angry, domineering men was either to accept them or to avoid them when I could, but until then, I didn't understand they were abusive. That word wasn't even a part of my vocabulary.

I once heard a saying that if you put a frog in boiling water, it will jump out, but if you put it in cool water and heat it slowly, it will stay and boil to death. That is abuse. My worst abuser charmed me and kept me comfortable until he knew he had my trust, and then he suddenly shattered it before I had a chance to realize that he was truly violent. By the time I understood my situation, I was physically broken and then completely and utterly depressed. When this man fractured my arm shortly after our wedding, I finally knew I had to get out, and so I began to quietly prepare to break free. First, I convinced myself that I could do it, then I planned my escape, which took a long time. I had to become mentally stable and physically able to deal with my abuser before I could get out. And just as important, I had to learn to speak up for myself, to seek help when I needed it, and to gain independence in my adopted country.

Even when I was thinking about escape, I didn't think of myself as someone who could stand on my own. I was in my early forties with three kids, with not enough education and nowhere to go. Even after I had left, it was hard to believe in myself or what I could do. Sometimes, self-discovery is lonely and sad. But it was certainly needed—it was my greatest accomplishment. And after numerous hours of self-reflection and much-needed therapy, I have learned the value of self-worth, such as trusting and believing in myself, and broken the cycle of abuse. The last thing I wanted was to become like my mother—stuck with a husband who did nothing but hurt her. So, I took my grandmother's advice—I made myself someone to believe in, and then, my best self became my truth. I went back to school and back to work, spent many hours with my kids, made new friends and strengthened old relationships, and made sure I had plenty of *me* time. Now I have an amazing career and an even more amazing story to tell. Finally, I have become the strong person I needed to be when I was younger, and now, I am helping others with what I have learned.

I wrote this book as a way of healing. Coming to America changed my life, as it has for so many others. Since I arrived in this country, I've learned important lessons about speaking up for myself, seeking help when I'm feeling low, and learning English and the skills needed to succeed in everyday life. With abuse, silence is not an option. Although my path took a while, finding my voice has set me free.

For anyone reading this book, it would make me happy to know my story could be a source of advice and inspiration to you, whether you were born in the United States or elsewhere. My sincere hope is that this book can touch your life and change your way of thinking, because writing it altered mine. The steps that I took to grow changed my life and gave me the success that I wanted.

I hope this story can inspire and help you find the aid you need. At the end of this book are resources for those seeking to escape abuse. If you are in an abusive relationship, just remember that the water may be boiling, but you can still get out of the pot. It's possible. I've done it.

MY FATHER'S HOUSE

My father was really two people. At home, he rarely took his hand off a bottle of vodka. During the day, he was a respected businessman, and when he was sober, he was a kind and loving dad. He provided a comfortable home for our large family and advised each of us to study and work hard so we could make something of ourselves in the future. He was a rather short man, no more than 5'6", and he always wore a baseball cap and a warm smile when he wasn't drinking. But when he came home from work, he would start drinking straight out of the bottle, which meant his calm, gentle demeanor would turn aggressive within minutes.

To this day, my memories of childhood are full of horrific images of my father repeatedly beating me and my nine siblings with his belt. For me, every day after school was a battlefield. Not knowing when or where my father would decide to strike me was terrifying. Since he was most likely drunk and there were so many of us, I wasn't the only one who dealt with his aggression. All ten of us kids and my wonderful mom would get the brunt of his anger when his nightly binge of alcohol consumed him. For the younger ones, it was especially hard. I clearly remember being around six years old and having my little baby brother hold on tightly to me whenever my dad entered the room.

Each day, he would leave for work early in the morning to open the store he owned in Los Jardínes, Santo Domingo, in the Dominican Republic. My father regularly attended church, and every day he got up early to run his store. He never started drinking until after lunch, but when he came home, the real drinking began. As the night wore on, his quiet, professional self would disappear while he drained his liquor. Then he would grab anything within reach—belts, hair brushes, or shoes—and smack anyone who got in his way. As bad as the hitting was, his drunken rants and the intense control he exerted over us were equally as scary. By the time I was about eight years old, he had me make his drinks and bring them to him. If I didn't hand him his drinks fast enough, or he didn't like the way my sisters and I did dishes, he would hit or yell at whomever was closest to him. Anything would set him off, and I dreaded coming home from school, fearful that his temper would flare in my direction.

My sober father was a serious man who always had a plan for everything he did in life. Everything could be an opportunity for a deal to him. He was often thinking up new business ideas, and he was a good provider of material things for our big family. When he was a young man, he was drafted to serve in the military for a short time, and after he was discharged, he had a brilliant idea: he opened general stores close to army bases for the wives and children of soldiers and allowed these families to open tabs they could pay at the end of the month. His stores became very popular, and we never had issues getting what we needed, even though there were so many of us. He managed for my entire family, all twelve of us, to have dinner together when he was home.

However, when he was on an angry, drunken tirade, our father would take our mother's spending money away from her and force my siblings and I to do our homework by candlelight, reasoning that he was the only one in the household who paid the electricity bill. He looked over my homework every night. It had to be completed, neat, and ready for presentation at the exact moment he demanded to look at my work. Even though I was a good student and completed my homework quickly, he never seemed to think I was good enough, and he repeatedly told me so.

Because of my father's stature in the community, my mom would never tell the priest about the abuse at home. While the neighbors may have heard my dad yell, no one knew how bad his drunken outbursts were or that he was hitting us. Even if they did know, there wasn't help available for us at the time. My mother knew of no organizations that helped families escape abuse; in our culture, abuse was not something that was acknowledged or discussed—it was hushed and ignored. We were afraid to speak up, and even if we had wanted to, there was no one we could tell. My father told us that our lives inside our home were private. Out of fear, we kept silent.

My glimmering hope back then was to look to my ever-so-patient and understanding *abuela* (grandmother), Rhafaela, for her wisdom and understanding. My grandmother was beautiful inside and out. She was a small, thin lady with light skin and short hair. I remember she had a smile ready for me whenever I would visit, and every time she spoke to me, my ears perked up to her words. My grandmother's wise advice guided me throughout my childhood and adolescent years and helped me to create a better life as a strong, independent woman. As the years passed, I was astonished by how much my grandmother's advice held true. For every possible scenario that affected my life, she not only knew the answer right away, but she explained it in such a pleasant way that I easily understood.

When I was little, my grandmother frequently told me, in her soft, comforting voice, "If you believe something, and you work hard, you can make it happen."

At that time, I believed in a lot of things—I believed (and still do believe) in God; I believed in love (and I still do), but like many people, I never really thought about believing in myself. As far as I was concerned, there were billions of others just like me, so I didn't think believing in myself was of great concern. My story was far from a fairy tale; I felt unimportant. In the meantime, my grandmother's passionate stories shored up my soul.

One of my favorite stories was how she met my grandfather, Fernando, when she was 19 and he was several years older. They met in the late 1940s in Paris, the City of Love, which was my grandmother's home. She told me that she was shopping in a small market near her home with her mother, my great-grandmother Stella, when she noticed a tall, handsome, young man navigating the busy stores, trying to purchase shower soap.

After a few glances at each other, he finally approached her. She told me that he was wearing a white Marine uniform, and he held his hat close to his chest. My grandfather was Dominican and spoke Spanish but very little French, so he carried a French–Spanish dictionary along with another book, some papers, and a few maps, which made his tourist status both obvious and touching to my grandmother.

For her, she said, "It was love at first sight." Once her eyes fell on him, she said that, in her heart, she knew that he was the man she was going to marry. From watching them together, I believe their love only grew stronger over the years. She told me that when Fernando, in broken French, introduced himself and shyly asked her for her name, she laughed and then responded by giving him her name *and* her address. It was a bold move at that time for a young lady to give a foreigner such personal information. She always told us she couldn't believe she did that. After a week of impatiently waiting to hear from him, Rhafaela finally found her Fernando knocking at the door. He was holding a single purple *Lavandula stoechas*, a Spanish lavender flower. They spent time together until his leave was over. She waited for her Spanish-speaking sailor, and when he completed his service to his country, he returned to marry her and take her to his island homeland.

Although it was hard to leave her family and her native France, my grandmother said her love for my grandfather led her to move with him to the Dominican Republic to start their family. They had two daughters: first, Luna Salome, and then my mother, Manuela. My aunt and my mother were very close. From their childhood through to this very day, Aunt Luna Salome has been my mother's support and confidant, and she has always been available to listen and advise our family and continues to be a comfort to us all.

The four of them lived happily in a small house with a balcony decorated with beautiful flowers, especially purple. Purple, my grandmother's favorite, was a blend of the two strongest colors: red and blue. She would tell me, "The color red represents happiness (like seeing the world through rose-colored glasses), and the color blue represents sadness (like being in a blue mood). When the two colors are combined, a certain balance is achieved, which is a lot like having a balanced life."

Paris had been balanced for her in many ways. The climate, she said, was "warm or cool, but never the extremes." It was a place "where everyone loved to walk or visit museums and the beautiful parks and gardens that were everywhere. There was always time for bread and coffee, or red wine." She smiled when she talked about France.

Her love and devotion to my grandfather, for her, was represented by the color red. The combination of red and blue gave her life harmony, she said, and she lived her life as if everything was purple.

I remember that my grandfather smelled slightly of cigars and always had a serious look on his face. He was loving and kind, but he was also very blunt when he needed to be.

My grandmother, on the other hand, was an extremely vibrant woman. She was excellent at cooking; the kitchen always smelled of casseroles and bread. I loved when she would let me help her make the salad. She loved her kitchen, which was small and bright. Her kitchen had a window with an oregano plant in it, and she insisted that she was the only one allowed to water it. I remember her cooking in the kitchen and constantly having to chase my hungry grandfather out, who would try to take a little bit of food before it was ready. She would scold and bicker with my grandfather lovingly. "Can you not wait a few more minutes until the food is done?" In my mind, they were the definition of love.

My grandmother was a source of inspiration in so many ways. She taught me to be strong and gentle at the same time. From her, I also learned my love of gardening. She grew lovely tropical flowers, daisies, bougainvillea, and Spanish lavender, her favorite. To this day, growing plants and flowers reminds me of her and makes me happy; I use it to help calm my anxiety.

Another lesson she gave was, "Always keep your chin up, and your eyes looking in front, no matter the situation." I still remember this today when I need a confidence boost. My grandmother's love and advice also gave my mother, Manuela, the strength to face tremendous challenges with grace. Their caring examples eventually gave me the courage to face my own fears and challenges.

Like my grandmother, my mother was strong and very smart. An incredible woman, she somehow managed to raise ten kids and handle my father's alcoholism and abuse all at once. To me, she had the heart of an angel. No matter how domineering and abusive my father had been the night before, my mother would always wake the next day with a positive attitude and a loving demeanor. She would serve the entire family a wonderful breakfast every day and show true concern for each of us on a bad day, even my father, who was often the cause. After breakfast, she would go over the meals she was planning on cooking for that day to make sure everyone liked the food she was preparing.

A truly beautiful woman, physically and spiritually, my petite mother carried herself very well and was always elegantly put together. She always wore lipstick and pearls, no matter what time of day it was, like many classy women of that time in the Dominican Republic. She had a sweet smell of vanilla that stuck to her skin and calmed the air around her. My mother was the gentle hand and warm heart against my father's rage and abuse. How she handled it, I don't know, but her advice to me was, "Always be mindful of your surroundings." It was good advice, and something I later learned to pay attention to, but almost too late.

She said to each of us, "If you can rise up from nothing each day, then tomorrow is nothing to worry about."

Before she married, my mother volunteered at our church and made a point to continue volunteering after she started her family. She had met my father at a concert when they were young. After dancing and talking the whole night through about their hopes and dreams, they fell in love. They both dreamed of a large family and talked of marriage. However, my father decided to join the military. While he was serving, my parents decided to wait to marry each other, and over time, they lost touch. After he was released, he came back to town, and just as soon as he got back, he found my mom, and they rekindled their relationship. They got married the summer of 1966. They had a small wedding at their church, and the reception was held in my grandma's backyard with family and friends. My mother was beautiful, and my father saw exactly what I saw as a child—that perfectly pressed, angelic figure who looked like she had never seen a bad day in her life, despite my father's instability.

Our paternal grandfather had passed away from alcoholism when our dad was young, but years later, we found out that our grandfather had a secret family. He was a hard man—a farmer who drank a lot of brandy and made my dad quit school to help in the fields. Like his own father, my dad also lived a secret life that I was unaware of until I was eight years old, when I was put in charge of doing his laundry. While cleaning his pockets out before putting his clothes in the washer, I found pictures and phone numbers on slips of paper in his pockets. A couple of years later, I learned who the people in the picture were when I discovered that I had two brothers outside of my parents' marriage. I was devastated, but I kept the secret for my mother's sake. The last thing I wanted was for her to find out about this. Later, I learned that she knew anyway.

When I was about nine years old, a bright-eyed, curly haired little boy was dropped off at our front door. It turned out he was our three-year-old half-brother, and my mother was being forced to raise him by my domineering father, who claimed he was worried about how the boy was being raised by his dishonorable mother.

My siblings and I were shocked at the new arrival, especially one whose presence brought shame to us and made us give up space for him in our crowded house (which was already filled with six girls and four boys sharing bedrooms, with only one-and-a-half bathrooms for the entire family) and, most of all, share our mom's attention. He was extremely shy and well mannered, but we told him there was no room for him and chose to ignore him at first, out of loyalty to our mom.

But our wise, caring mother reminded us, "Everyone be nice; he is your brother and a part of our family now. You need to make him feel welcome."

Following her lead, we gradually warmed up to him and eventually accepted him and learned to love him very much. Mom bought him a small bed of his own, but he ended up bunking with everyone in turn. He seemed to like being with his new, big family, with so many brothers and sisters to play with. Unfortunately, because he was in our father's house, he got beaten too, just like everyone else. After six years with us, he chose to return to his mother, but we have all remained close to him to this day.

Growing Up and Dreaming of Escape

Growing up, my older brother Poli and I were very close. Even though he had a lot of responsibility as the oldest in the family, he always made time for me. I remember him teaching me how to play baseball and how to ride a bike. We took walks often and spent any free time we could together. He was my best friend. I learned countless lessons from him too. He said the most important one was, "In baseball and in life, you have to stay focused and keep your eye on the ball." He never lost sight of that ideal.

When I think back on it, my big brother reminds me of the Greek god Apollo, god of protection. He always watched out for me and only picked fights when he knew he could win. Poli is a smart man, and he has worked hard to become who he is today, a respected lawyer in the Dominican Republic, and I am very proud of him.

My brother was always loving and protective, and I am lucky for that, considering that my father was such an angry drunk. When my father didn't get his way, he became enraged, so my brother and I hid his weapons for our own safety. Every time my father came close when he was angry, Poli stood in front of me, acting as a human shield. Our father and mother fought often, and it got so serious that on one awful occasion, he held a knife to my mother's throat.

He started screaming, "I own this house! I pay the bills!"

My mother begged for my dad to calm down and think about the children. Being only ten years old, I was certain he would kill my mother where she stood. I was frozen with terror at what was happening, but my brother jumped in between them. Suddenly, my dad softened, backed away, and set the knife down on the table as if nothing had happened.

On one of the worst nights, my dad stumbled in very drunk and surly. My baby sister slept in a crib in my parent's room. That night, when my dad came in, she started crying and crying. My mom tried to comfort her, but when she set her back in the crib, she wouldn't stop crying. I heard my dad yell at my baby sister, pick her up, and throw her to the floor.

My siblings and I heard my mother screaming and ran to the room where my baby sister lay very still on the floor. She had vomited and was unconscious. Leaving the rest of us children at home, my parents raced her to the hospital. The hospital staff thought she wouldn't make it. We frantically waited to hear how our sister was doing, but no one would tell us what was going on, just that she was in the hospital. After the incident, my father didn't remember what happened, and my mom didn't say anything. As always, we didn't know what we could do and were too afraid to ask questions. I wanted to tell someone, but I knew I could not. I knew if I spoke up I would get in trouble, so I kept quiet to keep the peace. I thought she was going to die that night, but thankfully, after two months, she recovered. When my sister finally came home from the hospital, her head was shaved and she couldn't hear out of her right ear for a long time. Today she is doing very well, but she has never had a clear memory of what happened that terrible night. For the rest of us, it was a night we would never forget.

Sadly, my mom had no help and no hope. It was a different time and a different culture. She had no other choice than to keep quiet about what was happening at home. A woman with ten kids could not leave them and or take them somewhere. On too many nights, we could hear her crying alone when she thought we were sleeping. My aunt Luna Salome, who was a smart, professional entrepreneur, as well as a wife and mom, did not like how my dad treated my mom. She would often try to persuade her to get out of her abusive relationship, because she wanted my mom to have a better life. As much as she loved her sister and appreciated her encouragement, my mom felt she had no choice but to stay. My dad never really seemed to like my aunt, which was hard on my mom because they have always been so close.

When we asked Mom years later, "Why did you stay?" she said, "I didn't know where to go, and I had to take care of you kids."

But as we grew up, each of us kids knew that we wanted out. We didn't want to end up in our mom's situation. Our dad was dangerous when he was drunk, and when he wasn't violent, he was pushy and verbally abusive. In his house, he was the king, and he put everyone down to make sure they knew it.

So as Poli and I, along with the rest of our siblings, grew older and stronger, we learned to dodge my father as much as we could by disappearing out of his sight, usually to our rooms. We also found out that because there were so many of us, there was safety in numbers. We realized he was growing older and more tired, and we could run faster. Us older children who had the "privilege" of making his drinks grew tired of the chore and the outcome. Eventually, we figured out that if we hid his belt and his liquor after he drank himself into a stupor, he would usually fall asleep before the beatings began.

Not all of my memories of my dad are bad. I enjoyed when he used to take us for ice cream on Sundays. One of the fondest memories from my childhood was when we would go to my Uncle Pablo's farm. Uncle Pablo was short and dark, with happy eyes, and he was always joking around and making us laugh. Even though he was older than my dad, he was naturally calm, maybe from being outside and doing what he loved, working around animals and nature. My uncle, his wife, and their two daughters lived on a farm that was four hours from the city, and on the way to his house, we would sing along to our father's favorite songs.

When we got to our uncle's farm, we would ride ponies and pick bananas and avocados. It was beautiful there, with lots of trees and greenery and so many stars visible at night. For us, going to our uncle's was exciting because it was the only time we had a chance to get away. Aside from the beauty of the farm, I thought the most memorable part of these trips was when our father and uncle would gather all the children for a songfest outside, usually around a campfire. Uncle Pablo was a very good musician who played his accordion at local events and clubs. When we came to visit, he would bring out his accordion, and our father would play the marimba, and we would dance to merengue music. As the night wore on, Uncle Pablo and our dad would tell funny and sad stories about their childhood and their father. This was very special to us because none of us children had ever gotten the chance to meet our grandfather. It was also good to see our father relaxed and enjoying being with Uncle Pablo and us.

In fact, the happiest my dad ever seemed was when he was with my uncle. I think he brought out the best in my dad. I can remember laughing and watching their eyes occasionally tear up as the night went on and they told their stories. Uncle Pablo wasn't like my dad. Being around our uncle, aunt, and cousins meant a lot to us kids because we were so close to them and to the farm. It was such a special place to us, filled with good memories. Every time we went, it felt like we were going somewhere far away, an almost magical place where we knew my dad was happy and loving to us.

Uncle Pablo would also visit us in the city. When he came, he would bring fruit for my mom. We loved having him around because of the change he brought out in our father. Uncle Pablo would often complain that the city was too noisy and try to convince my dad to move out of our house and purchase farmland.

While I was growing up, my mother tried her best to find each of us children something to focus on and invest our time in so we would not become too stressed by our home life. Poli's escape was baseball, and he did so well that he earned a scholarship to a private university. My escape was school, which I really liked, especially history. I also liked writing poetry and songs and singing in the church choir. And through constantly reading books, my mind became stronger and more independent. Because I was the oldest girl, it was my responsibility to read to my younger sisters, which I liked to do since it gave us time to spend together. I would also spend time brushing their hair, helping them with their homework, and anything else I could do to keep us close.

When I became a little bit older, my father asked me to work at his store. Sobriety at work did wonders for his personality. I was happy to be able to spend time with him when he was sober. He would talk to me about my plans for the future, and I would tell him about my dream of one day going to America, which he encouraged. He told me he liked the idea because he knew there would be better business and educational opportunities for me there. As a person who always had a plan for everything, my dad thought having a goal and working toward it was important, so he said if I did well and finished school, he would help me.

One of the reasons that I wanted to come to America was that I believed that it was a place where, "If you could dream it, you could do it." For as long as I could remember, I wanted to go to America more than anything, and I wanted to look and act the part. I would often go to the library with my good friend, Perla. We would go through American magazines looking at the fashionable ways the American people dressed. Perla and I would show pictures of American clothing to a friend of my mother's, who was a seamstress, and she re-created stylish looks for us that we could not find in the Dominican Republic. I remember asking her to re-create a pretty, green coat for me, and in it, I felt like a true American girl. I wore it often and wouldn't take it off, even when I was sweating in it from the heat.

Perla was my best childhood friend, and we have remained lifelong friends. Her warm smile and unique laugh have always brought me joy. Since I was shy, and my father kept my siblings and I close to home, I was lucky that she was my nearby neighbor. We walked to school together, talked, laughed, and shared each other's secrets. We did each other's hair, borrowed clothing, and told each other everything. More like sisters, we grew up together as family. We were so close, we could just look at each other and know what the other was thinking. I knew I could trust her completely, and while I was going through so much at home, she was consistently there for me, encouraging me.

SABELLA AND MY AMERICAN PLAN

My dream had taken hold, and as I was growing up, I was quietly trying to gain my freedom. To me, that meant America. In the meantime, I was a good student and studied hard. I also loved music, and my father would let me attend choir practice at church, which was my escape. I often wanted to make more friends, but I was too afraid of my father to defy him by socializing. He made it so unpleasant for our dates that I didn't really date in high school. If my sisters or I wanted to go out with someone, my dad would make the boy come to our house to meet him, and then he would sit on the couch between us and ask the boy questions. It was so uncomfortable with him sitting there in the middle that the boy wouldn't bother to come back. His dominating behavior, along with his drinking, meant most of us were too embarrassed to have friends over.

However, when I was 17, I met a man named Bruno, who was several years older and worked as a police officer. I had seen him on patrol around our neighborhood. My father and Bruno became good friends because he visited my dad's store frequently. He paid a lot of attention to me at the store, and my father gave him permission to ask me out. Bruno was older and self-assured, and I was very naive, but I craved freedom from my home life, so I agreed to go out with him. We started dating and spending time together. It was fun going out with him because we would ride around the town on his motorcycle, and I felt free. I was also happy to be getting out of the house—that is, until I became pregnant shortly after we started dating.

My family was shocked and unhappy with me, but my father was furious, to say the least. Thankfully, the hitting had stopped, but he did not forget to berate me and tell me how much I had let him down.

Apart from telling my family, the hardest part of my pregnancy was having to tell the clergy and the church members. Many people at the Catholic church where we attended were surprised when they heard. When I started to show, I chose to sit in the back of the choir, where I could not be seen, because I was so embarrassed. It bothered me that people treated me so differently. I felt bad and figured that everyone was upset with me, but one thing I knew was that I already loved my unborn child. During this time, I became more reserved and quiet because I was afraid of what others thought of me. At the beginning of my pregnancy, my grandmother was the only person who didn't turn her back on me. She protected me from my father and convinced the leader of the church choir to keep me in the group, even when I started to show. When my life was shifting around me, she was my rock.

Although I was pregnant, I still managed to finish high school, and not too long after I graduated, I gave birth to my beautiful daughter, Sabella. I had always liked the name Sabella because it sounded sweet. We decided it was the perfect fit for our baby girl. The entire time I was pregnant, I was nervous. I was so young, and I feared the responsibility of being a mom. I knew raising a child was going to be a lot of work, and I was not sure if I was ready.

The moment I gave birth to Sabella, though, I realized that even if I had not planned to be a mom at such a young age, I was grateful for the opportunity. From the first moment I got to hold my sweet little baby, I was in love. She weighed only six pounds and had dark eyes and curly hair. She was beautiful. I held her close and counted her fingers and toes. She was perfect. I was so excited to dress her in the beautiful outfits I had picked out for her. She was mine, and I was filled with happiness. My parents softened as soon as she was born. They took one look at her and fell in love.

Thankfully, my parents let Sabella and me stay in their home, and while I was there, I started taking night classes in a trade school. My dream was to work in tourism so I could interact with Americans on a daily basis. While I went to school, my mother happily watched Sabella. It was not easy leaving Sabella, even if it was only for a couple of hours. I spent all of my time with her, and being apart felt strange. I was a new mom and nervous to let her go, but I knew she was in good hands. My mom had raised me and my siblings wonderfully. I was so thankful to have my mom supporting me. She really wanted to see me finish my education and succeed in life.

My father always said he wanted what was best for me, and to him that meant seeing me go to college and get married. We would often sit on the patio and discuss my future while my father would have a drink. I know he hoped I would choose the more traditional path for my life. It took a while for him to accept the situation, but over time, he eventually offered to support me and my child. It was difficult at first, but in the end, I felt like my parents did their best to understand the situation.

Not long after Sabella was born, I moved in with Bruno. At first, I was happy to leave but also a little scared. While I did grow up cooking and cleaning, Sabella's father was rather controlling, and he wanted things done only his way. Simple tasks, such as cooking dinner, were overwhelming because of the pressure he would put on me to have them done right and in the exact time frame he desired. Bruno thought his uniform gave him the right to be arrogant, so it didn't take long before his true nature started coming out. He became verbally abusive and would sometimes hit me when he was displeased. On one very bad evening, when he had been drinking, he suddenly exploded, angry that the dinner I had cooked him that night was too salty. In rage, he tossed the TV through the window. I knew then it was time to go, so I put all that I could fit into a bag, called a taxi, and went to my parents' house.

I told my mother about the abuse I had been facing, and she said, "If you want to leave so bad, you have to leave. Don't be like me."

That night, Bruno came to my parents' house. He was yelling and screaming, saying he wanted to talk to me. My mother managed to distract him, allowing me and my brother Poli to sneak out and hurry to the police station for help. Soon, the police came to our house and arrested Bruno. My father showed up at the police station to pick me up just as Bruno arrived in custody. From across the station, Bruno yelled, "I know you will come back to me!"

I realized then it was time for action. Resolved to get away from Bruno and encouraged by my family, I went back to my parents' house to take care of Sabella and to complete school.

Fortunately, when I finished school, my father kept his promise to me to help me get to America. When my friend Perla found out that I would have the opportunity to go to America, we were both excited. My father lined up a job for me at the airport in Santo Domingo, which luckily was nearby the town I lived in. At the airport, I worked at the front desk. After one year of working there, I started to train as a flight attendant, and I ended up getting the opportunity to travel frequently to Texas for training. While I traveled, my mom took care of Sabella. Each time I visited Texas, I was sure to pick up something to bring back for Sabella, like small toys and American knickknacks, which she loved.

The time I was away varied. Sometimes it was a couple of weeks, and other times I would be in Texas for an entire month. During this time, I missed Sabella dearly, but I knew that I could not pass up the opportunity to have a good job and a chance to go to America.

The first time I visited America, all I had with me was a backpack containing pictures of Sabella, a CD player, and some personal items. One of my fondest memories was when I first stepped foot into the United States: I was listening to the uplifting song, "Las Cadenas" ("The Chains"), by my favorite singer, Selena Quintanilla. I sang along with the lyrics: "Me siento libre, me voy donde voy, y nadie lo impide, yo mando mi vida y me siento más feliz." (In English, it is: "I feel free, I go where I go, and nobody stops me, I'm in control of my life, and I feel happier.") The words felt timely and gave me hope. Selena inspired me and gave me strength through her music. Listening to her song, I was ready for my dream to come true.

Around the time I began to travel to the United States, Sabella's father moved to Puerto Rico. He would occasionally visit her, bringing her presents and taking her out to eat. While I traveled back and forth, my parents both took good care of Sabella for me. My best friend Perla was Sabella's godmother, and I felt better about being apart from Sabella knowing Perla would be there for her too. Sabella was my life and my reason for becoming the woman I am today. I wanted to give her a better life than I had in the Dominican Republic, and I knew that I could give her that if we got to go to the United States, which is why I became a flight attendant. I knew this job would give me more opportunities and allow me to provide for my daughter.

I also knew that if I stayed in Santo Domingo, I would fall into the same cycle of abuse as my mother, and so I left—to gain freedom and to be away from my father and from Sabella's father. There were hardships, especially when I missed my baby, my mom, my brothers, and sisters. But it was something I needed to do so that ultimately Sabella could have a mom.

THE DREAM TAKES A DETOUR

My nightmare really started in the early 1990s, when I was 22, after my dream of coming to America came true. I had spent the past four years doing everything I possibly could to make coming to America a reality. I didn't know it yet, but my dream of a perfect American life would be totally crushed—what I expected would turn out to be the opposite of my reality.

When I was in Texas working as a flight attendant, my father arranged for me to stay with longtime American friends of the family. They had visited the Dominican Republic often when I was growing up and would constantly visit my father's store. Over the years, they became like a second family. I was grateful when they opened up their home and let me stay with them.

After I had been training in the U.S. for a while and staying with this second family, they invited me on vacation with them to the "American West." I was very excited to travel to the Northwest to see the Rockies and visit the mountain towns nearby.

For me, a young woman who had only known the warmer climates of the Dominican Republic and Texas, a vacation to snowy regions sounded wonderful. It would also be another chance to chase my American dream.

As we drove, I looked at the beautiful colors, the mountain ranges, and the tall, thick, pine trees that surrounded us. I was amazed by the difference in the scenery from my island home.

One evening, we decided to stop for dinner at a restaurant popular for being a frequent dining spot of Kevin Costner—my all-time favorite movie star—and his crew while they were filming *Dances with Wolves*. Discovering this was the place where he filmed his famous movie was a treat for me.

While we were eating, the tall, blonde owner of the restaurant, Brian, approached our table, and he asked how we were enjoying our dinner. He paused and told me that I looked beautiful, even bundled up in a thick, bulky sweater and layers of warm clothing. I replied by telling him I wasn't used to the cold because I was from the Dominican Republic.

"Then what are you doing here?" he laughed. "It's getting colder by the day, you know."

I responded that I knew that the weather was changing quickly and told him that my friends and I were on our way back to Texas after the vacation was over. When I left, he came to the front, on the pretense of checking to make sure that I had paid. I noticed he kept looking at me, and that's when I realized something magical was starting to happen between us. We exchanged glances, then our phone numbers and addresses, and then smiles one more time before I left, but I didn't hear from him until I returned to Texas.

Then one Monday morning, very early, the phone rang. I was surprised because my family usually called me in the evenings, so I didn't know whom to expect on the other end of the telephone.

I answered with hopeful anticipation and said, "Hi."

Brian replied, "Hi," and then he spoke very rapidly. In fact, he spoke so fast, I, as a new English speaker, could hardly understand him. I asked him to slow down, and he responded not with a promise to slow his speech but with a request to see me. He wanted to come to Texas the next weekend. I checked first with the family I was staying with, and they were fine with the idea of Brian coming to visit, since they had already met him.

Brian arrived on Friday the next weekend. Night had already fallen when he drove up to the house. He was driving a silver convertible. He told me he rented the car for his visit with me, and he made sure I knew it had all the latest luxuries of the day. At the time, my thought was that he was trying to impress me. This opinion was confirmed when he said, with a cocky tone in his voice and a smirk on his face, "If you need to call your family, don't worry, I made sure to get a car phone." I was so tickled to see him, I ignored his overconfident attitude.

Even though his visit was very short, we got to know each other over those few days. We went out to restaurants; he came over to the house for dinner, and we spent time together when we went out. I didn't stay overnight with him because the family I was staying with disapproved of that idea very strongly.

However, even though we were not together the entire time, I was constantly on the phone with this wonderful new man in my life. It was like a fairy tale.

I watched him leave that Sunday; he was slowly waving his hand goodbye to me as he pulled out of the driveway. He had invited me to come visit him once more before I left for my home in the Dominican Republic.

A few weeks went by, and by this point, we were talking on the phone multiple times a day. Nearly every day, there was something new in the mail from him. There were often flowers or packages of cookies, and one day, a blue Columbia jacket arrived that I was to wear when I went back to the mountains to see him.

When I returned to Brian's town, I stayed in his home for ten days. He treated me like I longed to be treated, with respect and chivalrous behavior. He would make me coffee in the morning and open the door for me. For once, I felt special. One day, he took me to a museum where there was an entire area devoted to Kevin Costner. I loved seeing all the tributes to him. We got ice cream, he bought me some mementos from the museum, and we took some Polaroid pictures in the museum for each of us to keep in remembrance of our day together.

The trees began to turn to their majestic colors of yellow, red, and orange against the green pine trees as summer came quickly to an end. It was time for me to go home, but he begged me to stay with him and told me he loved me. "Stay with me," he pleaded.

I responded, "It's very cold here."

"I will keep you warm," he continued, trying to persuade me.

"And what about my daughter?" I asked.

"We will bring her here," he added.

I loved that idea. I was worried about my daughter missing me. Sabella was staying with my mom and dad in the Dominican Republic, and I wanted to get back to be with her soon. I had registered for her to start school before I left, and I had sent her school supplies and a new outfit. She was really looking forward to seeing me again. I wanted to be there for her because I knew that this was a significant time in her life. I told him I was planning to go back to Texas to finish my flight attendant training, then returning home to the Dominican Republic to be with my daughter because I missed her so much. I was eager to finish the on-site training so I could go back home and be with her more frequently during the more flexible part of the training. As long as I remained in the program, I could travel back and forth between the Dominican Republic and the United States.

Brian replied by telling me that if I stayed with him now, he would go with me to bring her back from the Dominican Republic. I wanted to stay, but even though he was saying all the right words, life doesn't always cooperate with what we want. And I knew how much more I wanted to return to my daughter. Sadly, I told him I had to leave.

His words in response stuck with me for a long time. He said, "Don't leave. I love you." I was surprised but delighted to hear those words because I also had feelings for him.

What could I do? I thought and thought about my feelings for him and for my newly acquired love of the pretty town and the unending high hills surrounding it, which were so incredibly different from my home in the Dominican Republic. After hours of thinking about his words and his love for me, I told him I loved him back and that I would stay with him if he promised to help me get my daughter and bring her back to live with us. He agreed and returned with me to Texas to help me pack my things so we could come home to the beautiful landscape, clear streams, deer, pheasants, elk, and bison. Being there was like a dream. I loved the beauty of the open spaces.

After giving Brian my promise, I returned to the Dominican Republic to see my daughter a few days later. Sabella was beyond excited for me to return. When I was gone, we had talked on the phone constantly, and I often sent her packages in the mail with books or toys or a little bit of money whenever I could afford it, but nothing compared to actually getting to see her in person. I told her about the man I had met and our plan to bring her back to the U.S. so we could be together.

At this point, Sabella was almost six years old and was becoming very inquisitive. We discussed her coming to live with us in the States, and she agreed that this was a good idea. She had never seen snow in her own backyard, and when I told her about how cold and snowy it was, she immediately told me that she wanted to come to America and experience it. I told her how the animals I had seen in America were unlike those in the Dominican Republic, and she was intrigued. I told her I would work to bring her there soon. She was disappointed that she couldn't go right away. In the meantime, she would stay with my parents and see her father often because he had moved back near my parents. It broke my heart knowing I would be leaving her again, but after having seen America, I knew it would be best to work to bring her there. I worried she would think that I was leaving her in the Dominican Republic because I wanted to, not because I felt I had no other choice. My biggest fear was that she would forget me, so I did everything I possibly could to remain in her life even though I was miles away. I promised her that I would work my hardest in order for us to be together.

While visiting, I also got to see Perla. We always shared our dreams and our plans no matter where we were. Even though we talked by phone at least once a week, it was so good to see her in person again. I told her about Brian and showed her a picture of him. She thought he was very handsome. She was glad to see me happy and full of hope for my future. She encouraged me and the American dream we shared. Because she had family in the U.S., I knew she would eventually move, and she did. Fifteen years ago, she moved to New York and married a nice guy. My family goes to see her when they visit the U.S. She is still very stylish, but now she dresses in the latest fashion trends instead of just looking through American magazines and dreaming about coming here, like we did as girls.

At the end of my trip to the Dominican Republic, I returned to Brian's home in America. The day I left, I hugged Sabella about a thousand times and reassured her that I would call her often and do everything I could so she could come live with me. I knew she was well cared for by my family and that her father, even though I was not very fond of him, loved her very much and was there for her. It was upsetting to leave because I knew that Sabella didn't just need her father or her grandparents or aunts and uncles, she needed her mother. I went back to America determined to find a way for Sabella to live with me. My family responded well because they knew I was happy and how much I wanted to make a place for Sabella. The town where Brian lived was a charming, small place where everyone knew one another and made newcomers like me feel welcome. He lived in a large house on the top of a hill on the edge of town, and I spent many days looking out at the entire town from the balcony of his home.

Brian and I spent every possible minute together. I started working for him at his restaurant. I was still learning new words in English, but I did very well at my job and enjoyed interacting with my customers, which helped me practice my language skills. Fortunately, I had my work visa, and I was already adjusted to the American culture due to working at the airport and my flight attendant training. I was happier than I had ever been; I had a new job and a wonderful man who said he loved me and who treated me like I deserved to be treated. This was the first time I had ever experienced a man caring for me like he did.

I had even made a couple new friends. Working alongside of me at the restaurant was Vivian, a bubbly, outgoing woman who befriended me. Although she was often a little too flirtatious with some of the customers, she and I got along well. While I was working on my English skills, she would help me with my pronunciation, and in return, I would teach her some words in Spanish. Vivian was from Florida, so she grew up around a lot of Spanish speakers. She said being around me made her feel at home. I had a lot of fun working with her. Another girl I met was Lucecita. She was from Peru and was so good to me. I came to love her like a sister. We met when she visited Brian's restaurant to have dinner. I was her server, and we hit it off right away. Lucecita was my only friend there who spoke fluent *español*. A small lady, she had very bright eyes and high cheekbones and stood only about 5' 2" and weighed only 105 pounds. She always had a way of making others feel welcome, no matter the situation.

Life was beautiful, and it seemed like I had entered a new chapter in my life. I loved every moment of every day, and I especially loved that we had started the paperwork to bring my daughter to the United States. We were waiting for the clearances for her to come to the U.S. and for permission from her father. I felt stable for the first time in years.

A few months after I moved in with Brian, I became very sick and decided to get a checkup. After running tests, the doctor told me the issue. I was so relieved! I wasn't sick. I told Brian the news: I was carrying his child. At the time, I was about four weeks pregnant and thought he would be happy because we were so in love.

When I told Brian the good news, his first response was combative, verbally attacking me. He was angry that I had not taken enough precautionary steps to not become pregnant. His response shocked me; I thought he would be excited. He said harshly, "Well, on Monday we can go and take care of that." I was stunned. I had thought he loved me and we would be together based on how he had treated me up until that very moment.

His response confused and upset me because he had not raised his voice to me before, and I didn't understand what he was trying to say—my English still wasn't very good at that time. I asked what he meant by this, and he told me that he wanted to "cure" me of my pregnancy.

I was shocked. "I can't do that. I just can't." How could he ask me to do what he was suggesting? How could I do anything but refuse!

His comments will stay with me for the rest of my life. He told me coldly, "I can't let you have that child. I can't get involved in a long-term relationship like this. If you keep this child, *you will have to go.*"

My choice to be with him on my journey to America was becoming a bad dream, and on this new turn, I had no hints for guidance on which path to follow.

I was upset and hurt that Brian could treat me like this. I was both sad and angry that Brian did not want me to have the baby. I can remember crying myself to sleep thinking about having to give up my baby. I felt so much pain and anxiety. Brian was so sure in his decision that we would not be keeping the child. He made me feel so small, like I had no control, which led me to become depressed. It did not help that I was away from my family and friends. Lonely and worried, I called my friend Perla in the Dominican Republic and reached out for advice on what to do. I asked her not to tell anyone there about what I was going through. I was scared to tell my family, especially my dad. I knew they would be disappointed. I valued her opinion and knew I could trust her to keep my secret. Although Perla said she could not advise me on the choice I should make, she urged me to make the decision that felt best for me and for my baby.

One of the hardest parts was being forced to make this decision alone. I felt so weak trying to grieve the pain that Brian had caused me. So I asked myself, *Do I take the road to the right and keep this gift from God that is growing within me, or do I take the road to the left and satisfy Brian's wishes?* My choice became quickly obvious to me, and that choice was the life of my child. I loved Brian, but I knew that I loved my baby more. I had already been apart from my daughter for too long, and I was not going to lose another child, whom I knew I already loved dearly. I began to pack my things and to start my journey alone.

Moving out and leaving Brian was not an easy task, emotionally or physically. It was hard to get out of bed. I still had terrible morning sickness, and I was in constant mental and emotional turmoil. Brian tried to help, but when he did, he didn't say much at all. Since I had known him, he had been quiet about discussing what he was feeling, but I could tell this decision was hard for him. What I didn't understand was why he did it anyway. I was constantly crying, unable to control my emotions. I loved him. I hated his choice, but I still loved him, and I was in shock for days. I didn't understand how a man could abandon a woman carrying his own child, especially after he had told me to stay and had asked me to leave my family to be with him.

My saving grace was Lucecita. She and her husband, Harold, had no children, but she was loving and motherly to me. Her name, Lucecita, means little light, and she was definitely my light and my support. She always had a way of making me feel a little bit better, even though I was constantly feeling depressed. It was difficult to find the courage and motivation to get back on my feet. I felt low and discouraged about my situation. It seemed like each step I took caused me even more pain. In the midst of the difficulties I was facing, Lucecita helped me with every task, from lifting the boxes that I could not bring myself to remove from the house, to making phone calls to people or organizations that could help me with the baby, to even finding me a small apartment for when the baby was born.

When I became pregnant, I was still working for Brian at his restaurant. When the relationship ended, I needed a new job. I started working right away, including a full-time job at a grocery store and a part-time job at a women's clothing store, where I worked evenings and weekends. The apartment that Lucecita helped me to find was near the grocery store, so I walked to work. I walked everywhere because I couldn't afford a car, but I enjoyed the exercise. Everyone at the small grocery store was nice to me. There were only ten people on the staff, and most of them had been there a long time, but they made me feel comfortable. We would bring in snacks to share during our breaks. I got to know the customers too, who were just as friendly as the staff.

Shortly after I started working there, I met Lemuel. He became a good friend, one who would change my life. I noticed he was a bit sweaty when he came in one night to get something quick to eat and drink. When he came to my register, I asked him if he had just worked out, and we struck up a conversation about exercise and working out, since it was something I had loved to do before I became pregnant and walking became my daily exercise. Since he came in regularly, we usually talked, so when he started joking around and flirting with me, I laughed and told him, "Don't get too flirty with me, I'm pregnant." He looked surprised since I was only a couple of months along, but he laughed too, and from that day on, we became close friends.

Lemuel would often walk me to my apartment when I worked at night, and on snowy nights, he would wait for me to get off and would drive me someplace to get a cup of tea and talk. Lemuel's looks were in such contrast to his personality. He was large in build and very muscular, but his gentle demeanor contrasted to his looks. He was always calm and very caring. It was so good to have a friend like him to talk to.

During this time, Lucecita helped me with my apartment. Considering that she could not have kids, she was absolutely delighted that a child was coming into her life! Like any close friend would do, she helped me with everything. We decorated my small apartment until it became my home, and she taught me the ins and outs of the town. She provided fresh flowers and a new bassinet and crib for my son or daughter's homecoming.

Her husband, Harold, painted the walls in happy, primary colors: blue, deep red, and bright yellow. It felt like home.

Everything was perfect and ready for my beautiful baby, yet I was overwhelmed with stress, work, and my future child! I was worried about how I would take care of this gift from God inside me. Although I was not officially diagnosed then, I believe I fell into a severe state of depression during this time. Slowly but surely, over a course of months, I had developed several signs of deep depression. Over time, my hair started to fall out, my appetite diminished, and my skin began to shrivel. Additionally, throughout the pregnancy, my mouth was quite parched from not acquiring enough nutrients for myself and for my future child. During this time, I had no contact with Brian, which made me feel abandoned and sad. I think being far from my home and Sabella while carrying a baby all by myself sent me spiraling downhill into deep sorrow.

As the months went on, my health declined as my distress increased, and I started to fear the possibility that my baby might not survive the pregnancy. The doctor was also concerned, and unfortunately, my baby became a bit eager to see the world—almost three months too eager.

MY LEONARDO—ALMOST MINE

One day, when I was almost seven months pregnant, I was working at the grocery store and started to feel my head grow light and my feet grow heavy. I tried to keep calm as I scanned the items, but I was losing my focus and starting to panic. I became dizzy, and the next thing I knew, I was a thousand feet in the air, flying over the high, Western plains in an emergency airlift to a hospital in a larger city, almost two hundred miles away from my adopted town. I had apparently fainted. Thankfully, the customers in the grocery store noticed and immediately called 911.

After arriving at the hospital via helicopter, I found myself lying in a bed, covered with a white blanket, with my feet up in stirrups and no idea of what was happening around me. The doctors and nurses tried to explain what was going on, but my English was still far from perfect, and I was frightened by the strange surroundings and people I didn't know. I asked them to speak a little slower to me after a quick discussion about what was happening. I was very confused; after all, I was barely seven months pregnant. I didn't even realize I was in labor.

After some discussion with the hospital doctor, I finally realized that I was in early labor, as unfortunate as that was. However, I assumed that I would return to the town where I was living to have the child, or if I had to stay where I was, that the C-section would be scheduled for a later date. I was taking medication in the hospital to delay my labor, so I thought that maybe the baby would grow and develop just a little more before I had it. But this did not turn out to be the case.

After three days, the contractions still continued to increase, and the doctors decided to put me to sleep for an emergency C-section. After waking up, I felt groggy at first. Confused, upset, and high from pain medications, I begged for information. I knew I had delivered my baby, but I had no idea where the baby was, if it was healthy, or what sex it was. I suddenly felt alone, and the room became dark and gloomy.

When I awoke again, the medical staff wouldn't let me get out of bed. I couldn't communicate because of my limited English and the medications, which slowed my thoughts. The nurses tried to explain what had happened, but I had so much trouble understanding them. They were speaking so fast. My only thoughts were about my child. I didn't care that my insides were quite literally stitched together at this point, or that I was still on IVs and monitors. I didn't think about myself. I needed to know about my baby.

Lucecita came to visit, and she interpreted for the doctor and me. Everything came into focus eventually—I had given birth to a boy via emergency C-section a few hours prior. I would have wanted to have been awake, despite the pain, to experience my baby coming into the world. Sadly, I had missed that, but I was relieved to learn I was going to see him for the first time the very next morning. They had even scheduled a nurse to come pick me up, so I didn't have to walk. I was so excited that I couldn't sleep that night. Lucecita and I talked for most of the night in rapid-fire conversation in Spanish. I couldn't contain my excitement, and I couldn't stop smiling, thinking about meeting my child.

The nurse came in the room the next morning. She helped me into the wheelchair so I could go and see my son. Lucecita walked next to me as I was wheeled down the hallway. She held my hand the entire time.

When we arrived at the NICU (neonatal intensive care unit). I could see that there were more babies in incubators than I could have ever imagined possible, and I had no idea which baby was mine. It was amazing to me that so many women had early births so close to mine. It was sad to see, but incredible to look at those little miracles. They were so small and so cute. The nurse pushed me to my child's incubator, and I saw his small features for the first time. He was completely hooked up to machines, IVs, and monitors, and even though his face was the only part of him I could see clearly, he was beautiful. I found out that Leonardo was born with sleep apnea, meaning he would sometimes stop breathing while sleeping. This was a very serious condition, and because of it, he had to wear a special monitor, even after he left the hospital. He looked almost bluish in color and weighed about four pounds, so his tiny frame looked long and skinny, but he was still beautiful to me. He looked like me. He was mine. I named him Leonardo the moment I saw him.

Naturally, this was when I began to ask questions about Leonardo's health, and Lucecita translated. I found out that I was supposed to leave the hospital in two days, but my child, even though he was doing well, would stay indefinitely. I dreaded returning to my apartment because it was a few hours away from the hospital, which meant it would be impossible to visit Leonardo every day. Once more, I felt like I was being kicked out, but this time I was a mother again, with a newborn son that I could not take with me.

Later that evening, Brian showed up in the hospital room. I saw him poke his head into the room and smile a little. I smiled back. I thought he had come back for me, that he cared! He was even asking about my day and what had happened to land me in the hospital almost three months too early. He showed genuine interest in my child, and it felt so amazing and comforting to see someone I knew. Then he walked in the room, and I saw someone following him—my friend from the restaurant, Vivian. I couldn't believe it! Someone else had cared enough to drive the three hours down to see me! I thanked them for coming. But then I noticed an odd look on Brian's face, and suddenly, I knew what was going on. They were together! Apparently, she and Brian were now dating. I was crushed. I couldn't believe that Brian had moved on so fast and that he was now dating a friend that I thought I could trust. I felt angry and sad. I now realize that being angry at Brian was only hurting myself.

They had decided to drive to the hospital and see how I was doing after hearing I had gone in labor early, or so they claimed at the time. Thinking on it now, I realize that the only reason he was there was for the child, and not for me.

I was alone that night. Brian and Vivian had left my side, and Lucecita had left to go home for a while to rest. I knew nobody around me, and shadows of unfamiliar people danced through my room as they passed by my hallway window. I did a lot of thinking and a lot of praying. I prayed for hours. I cried. The shadows came and went, but I was still there. I didn't have my baby inside me or beside me. I thought a lot about how I was going to get him home. I wondered when it could happen. I needed someone, anyone, to talk to. I begged God for company.

There were times throughout the pregnancy when my faith wavered. I never gave up on God, but there were moments when I wondered if He was truly there for me. But then, three nuns arrived at my door, dressed in full habit. To me, they smelled like cookies and warmth in the cold winter. I was no longer alone. He had answered my prayers the day after my son was born.

They talked to me in English. They asked me questions about my life, my baby, and the dad. We talked for a very long time. The nuns would sometimes look at each other with mournful uncertainty, unsure of what would happen to me. Though they tried to hide their concern, I could feel it, and in my darkened room, I could see it on their kind faces illuminated by the cool glow of hospital lights shining through the window. I knew that my situation was not ideal. Since I grew up Catholic, nuns were a familiar presence to me; however, the anxiety about my situation crept into my soul.

Even though I did not know these particular nuns, they talked to me like I was their friend, their sister, and God's child. They treated me with respect and compassion. I requested a prayer, and they stood next to my bed and prayed. They prayed in the name of the Father, the Son, and the Holy Spirit for my child and for me.

They started to leave the room (my guess was that someone else needed them), but in desperation, I asked them to continue, and they did for my sake. In the middle of another recitation of the Lord's Prayer, one of the nuns began to speak it in Spanish. Her voice was soft and comforting in this harsh and complicated situation. It was as though God had put the words into her mouth. It sounded heavenly to me.

The nun had not given any indication that she spoke Spanish before that moment. She had only spoken proper English to me, so there was no hint of her ability to speak my language. But there it was. Her words in my language became my lifeline. In somewhat fractured Spanish, she told me about a place I could stay while Leonardo got stronger, called the Ronald McDonald House. It wouldn't cost as much as the travel to and from my town, and because I was just out of surgery (the C-section), it was important for me to move as little as possible. I could rest easy and see my child. It seemed perfect. They gave me the information about the Ronald McDonald House, then said goodbye. I thanked them a thousand times.

I woke up the next morning ready to see Leonardo again, but I was hurting. The medicine was wearing off, and I could feel each individual stitch in my stomach. I was alone again. I was scared, and I was unprepared to leave the hospital. I had no boots or winter clothes, just a pair of tennis shoes against a foot of snow.

When I was discharged, the doctors told me I needed to start walking again to regain my strength. Before I was going to go, I was getting to see my son. Walking at a snail's pace through the hallways of the medical facility, I returned to the NICU. I arrived at Leonardo's incubator and was so excited to be able to touch his tiny purple feet for the first time. I looked at his nail beds—they were blue, and he was small and frail. Even though he was so tiny, I was content touching his little feet, and to me, he was just right.

The NICU nurse in the room told me he was doing very well, considering the circumstances. She went on to tell me that I could hold him gently for the first time if I wished. I excitedly agreed. I asked her if I could breastfeed him, and she told me, "No, because he was so premature, he does not know how to be fed just yet."

I was rather upset about this, knowing that feeding my child was a bonding experience for us, but I also knew that it was important to listen to what the nurse said. She explained that I would need to pump and save milk for little Leonardo so he could be fed through a tube. And though I was disappointed by this, nothing could take away the feeling of excitement that I had from knowing I could hold my baby.

I sat down in a rocking chair and felt heavenly peace as the NICU nurse placed little Leonardo in my arms for the first time. I held him for about 20 minutes. I never lost focus on my baby boy. He breathed slowly but surely. He fit so perfectly in my arms. I was concentrating on the moment—I never wanted to forget this. I didn't even hear the approaching footsteps of the man who was suddenly standing in front of me. But when I looked up, there he was. He was well dressed and official looking, but I can distinctly remember his brown boots, still wet from walking through the winter snow.

He asked, "Is your name Argentina?" Although I had a strange feeling, I tried to stay collected.

I replied cautiously, "Yes, sir, how may I help you?"

He looked at me intently as he handed me a thick stack of papers that I knew I had no hope of understanding. While holding my precious baby, I tried my best to read it. I glanced at the paper, trying to understand what was happening. There were words that jumped off the page and stuck in my memory, and I suddenly became very fearful. Words such as "stay away," "custody," "the child's father," and "DNA" burned in my memory and scarred my brain. The same man who previously hinted that he wanted to do away with my baby before he was born was now going to take him away from me. While I was giving birth, Brian had filed a restraining order and had somehow gotten custody of Leonardo. Considering the situation and his previous attitude about having a baby, why he wanted to do this, I didn't know. But he did.

My heart was breaking as I looked at Leonardo's little face. The man who had handed me the papers attempted to comfort me by saying he was sorry, but I was upset and scared. Leonardo was sleeping peacefully on my chest. I kissed his forehead and then gave him back to the kind nurse. I carefully pushed myself out of the rocking chair and stood slowly. The whole world was spinning around me like I was on a roller coaster. I couldn't believe the terrible thing Brian had done. He had taken Leonardo from me. The man who wanted to "cure" me of my pregnancy now wanted the baby.

Despair and fear rushed throughout my entire being. I could not keep my composure anymore. Sickened and crazed with anguish at Brian's betrayal and the loss of my newborn, I broke down. And then I began running. I ran down the long hospital hallway.

As I ran, I could feel the stitches and my heart quickly snapping. I ran faster than I thought I could, even with my stomach opening. Consumed by hopelessness, I could hear myself wailing and crying as I ran.

I don't remember much after that, because I began to have a panic attack. I was immediately rushed back into a hospital room and given medication to calm me down. After having the panic attack, I was completely and utterly devastated. They re-admitted me so they could restitch my wound. I thought I'd never see my baby again. I was crushed.

Once I was discharged from the hospital a day later, I knew that the Ronald McDonald House was still the right place to stay. Staying there allowed me to feel close to Leonardo even though I was not allowed to see him. His father had put a restraining order on me, and I had no way around it, though I tried. I went to the hospital every day for two weeks and asked about him. They told me nothing. They said, "We are no longer allowed to tell you that information." Their hands were tied. But even though my heart was shattered and I didn't have much hope, I still went, and I still asked.

One day, I spotted the nurse who had helped me in the NICU, and I knew that she was my only ticket to knowing something, *anything* about Leonardo. I begged her for any information about my baby. She paused to think, and even though we both knew that she was supposed to keep quiet about the situation, she revealed that he was going to be leaving soon and that he was much better.

"Go home. Go back home," she said to me. "Find a lawyer. There are people that will help you." She shook her head and then looked at me with sad eyes. "I hate what happened to you. My heart hurts."

Grateful to know at least that Leonardo was improving, I called Lucecita and Harold to come pick me up and take me back to my little apartment so many miles away. There I was, riding in the back of a Jeep, watching the blizzard around me fold onto the ground, snow on snow. We talked about what the plan was going to be when I returned home.

Lucecita's husband, Harold, told me in a very stern voice, "Don't get your hopes up." He then explained himself by saying, "We must consider that Brian, the father of your child, is very powerful and well known in town. To win, he will hire the best lawyer. He will fight tooth and nail for a child he didn't even want."

I knew Lucecita's husband wasn't trying to be hurtful, but the conversation only worsened my mood. My only goal was to get my child back, and I felt lost on how to accomplish this. My feelings of sadness, despair, and anxiety grew stronger with each mile.

It seemed like we were on the road forever, but we had only been driving for a few hours. When I entered the apartment, it felt so empty, even though it was still decorated and waiting to welcome my child. I remember walking around his room and feeling devastated. I had purchased sheets with cars on them for his crib, and it hurt to know that he would not be sleeping there. I remember looking at his dresser and seeing the two stuffed elephants I had gotten for him and thinking to myself that he would never get to have them. It hurt me imagining that Brian would get to be the one to purchase Leonardo stuffed animals and tuck him in at night, and that I was stripped of my right to be his mother. Everything was the way I had left it, but hope had left the room. There was no baby in the little bassinet in the corner; my heart was miles away with my newborn.

My friends wanted to stay with me for the night to comfort me. I looked them in the eyes, understanding their good intentions, but I was unreachable in my despair and told them coldly, "Do me a favor—please just leave." I knew I needed time by myself to cry and to grieve. They respected me and the intensity of my sadness, and they left.

After they were gone, I tried to walk around as the colors on the wall grew dimmer. Feeling empty and disconnected from my baby and from the world, I asked questions into the dark: "Is this real? Am I dreaming or hallucinating?" But I knew I wasn't—the stitches in my belly and my broken heart told my entire story. Leonardo was there, and then he was gone. It *was* real. It did happen. I had not only been unable to be with my daughter, but now I was apart from my son. Both of my children were far from me, and I felt powerless and heartbroken.

I lay thinking on the floor for hours and hours. In a daze, looked at the ceiling, staring straight up at the light until my eyes burned. I was trying to come up with a plan. The thoughts darting through my mind were very scary to me. I had never felt so angry or so powerless in my entire life. I needed that power back, somehow. So many irrational ideas ran through my mind, completely crazy thoughts I never imagined I'd think. Delirious with grief and fear for my child, my thoughts swung wildly out of control. *What if I kill Brian? What if I kill myself after that? What if I steal my child back? What if I run away?*

Hours passed as the distraught thoughts continued to race through my mind. Nonetheless, I knew they were impossible, and my hopelessness sank heavier in my heart.

All these desperate thoughts swirled in my head, and as I thought, the image of *mi dulce abuela* (my sweet grandmother) Rhafaela came to mind over and over. At this point, because everything had happened so abruptly, I had not even told my family that I was pregnant, let alone that I had delivered my child. My parents didn't know that their first grandson even existed. I was so alone, but my grandmother was there for me in spirit. It felt like she was holding a conversation with me. She told me to stay calm. She told me to think like she would in this situation. And I knew that no, she would never kill anyone, including herself. And no, she would never steal anything or anyone and run away. I had to think of a new plan, a rational one.

Calmer now, I got up and walked a few steps to the kitchen to get a glass of water to cool myself off. I looked over at the blinking red light on my answering machine that sat on the table nearby. The message box was full. I pushed the "Play Messages" button, and voices started to come out of the speaker. Many of the voicemails were from my friend Lemuel.

While I was in the hospital, he had called often, leaving messages, wondering where I was and if I was okay. I called him back. He said I didn't seem like myself on the phone, so he decided he would come over to my apartment to talk and to keep me company. He was worried, but he sounded relieved to hear my voice. I didn't have the strength to tell him what had happened.

He knocked on the door, and like a sleepwalker, I answered. His excitement and happiness for the apparent homecoming of my child was soon met with confused frustration when he saw the empty crib across the room. He realized I had delivered the baby. He looked at me and asked what had happened. I couldn't hold my feelings or the story back any longer. I told him everything, and I pleaded with him to find a way to help me get my baby back. He then looked at me with confusion and sadness. He was as scared about the awful situation as I was, but he told me he was confident that he could change my luck, and he smiled a little.

He said gently, but firmly, "I will do whatever it takes. I promise I will help." He told me outright that he needed nothing from me. I could not have been more grateful.

FIGHTING FOR LEONARDO

We talked for hours. We made plans, even talking about possibly escaping to a Native-American reservation so that nobody could find Leonardo and me. I was so worried about getting my son back that I even considered this. After moving to the area, I had gotten to know a lot of Native Americans who made me feel welcome. Many of them were regulars at the grocery store where I worked, and they often visited the restaurant. While I knew in my heart that the Western tribal members would help me, I also knew this plan would not work forever. If I moved to the reservation, I would never be able to see my family again. Moving to the reservation could have also been harmful for Leonardo because of his health problems. At this point, however, I was desperate and willing to consider almost anything.

After talking about many of our options, Lemuel said, "We will have to think of a more permanent plan, Argentina. What that man did to you was wrong, and we *are* going to get your child back. How about this: you go take a shower and relax, and I'll go get us something to eat. I'll be right back, and we will keep discussing ideas."

Lemuel opened my blinds before he left. As I looked out the window, I saw the cold world around me. The snow was still falling. Even though it was below freezing, I felt like someone was holding my hand with a warm touch. I felt better knowing I was no longer so alone, thanks to him. He left, and when he returned, we sat in my living room and discussed ideas over soup.

"I have another plan." I said. "I can gather up money from people I know and hire a good lawyer. I can even sell my things, including my grandmother's jewelry. It isn't like I need them right now anyway."

Lemuel shook his head no. He let me down gently, saying that my idea would cost more money than we could ever come up with. He suggested speaking to an attorney. I decided to take his advice and set up a meeting with a state legal aid lawyer.

The thought of telling my family crossed my mind then, but I pushed it away. I wasn't ready yet. I know they could have helped me, but I felt I needed to do it on my own. I did not want them to know that I had failed or that I had been pregnant and alone.

I was lucky that the lawyer I received had a big heart as well as a big brain; he was willing to help for many hours that I could not pay him for. We worked every day so I would be prepared for the court date. The three of us, Lemuel, the lawyer, and I, put our heads together and collectively thought of new ways of getting Leonardo back. The meetings, while productive, were very frustrating for me. I was the mother of this baby—was this not enough?

The lawyer often said that we should not get our hopes up, considering the power that Brian had, the money he had invested in this case, and the problem with my immigration status (I was in the process of renewing my visa). He was right, and I understood that he was not trying to hurt me in any way; he was being preemptive and trying to spare my feelings if things did not go my way in court. Though I never got my hopes up, I also refused to lose sight of my goal. We had two months to prepare my case for Leonardo.

The court date seemed to come quickly. Lucecita and Lemuel sat behind me in the courtroom. Before I entered the courthouse, Lucecita took my hand and told me to remain cool and stay calm. "Just listen to what the judge has to say," she explained in Spanish, so I completely understood. I nodded.

I sat down in the courtroom and looked around. It was my first time in a courthouse, and I was nervous. Everything had a dark brown wood or brick red color to it. It felt official, which only made me more terrified. The room was dry, and the air felt thick with tension at the same time.

I heard footsteps from behind me. Looking back, I saw a face framed with thick, heavily dyed black hair, the face of a person whom I had trusted as a friend, Lucas. He was someone I had met through Brian. We had been very close, and he used to visit the restaurant almost every night for dinner. He would also often hang out with Brian at his house. Sometimes Brian and I would go out for a beer or even go out dancing, and Lucas and Vivian would join us. He was Brian's best friend. Usually he was casually dressed, but in court, he wore a white, button-down shirt under a thick, woven, brown suit with white socks under tacky black shoes. His attire was completely mismatched, and he walked like he was uncomfortable, as if his shoes didn't fit correctly. Maybe he just knew what he was about to do was wrong. I looked at Brian, who was sitting next to his lawyer; we barely made eye contact.

Lucas took the stand for Brian's side. He stood before the judge, lawyers, the witnesses, and me and swore on his honor to tell the truth. I could not believe what he said then. He was lying before he even said a word. At that moment, I looked him dead in the face and squinted at his shifty eyes and pursed lips. Brian's lawyer started asking Lucas questions about me, and he responded robotically.

"She is bad. She is a bad mom. She would not take good care of Leonardo. We, as a state and as a nation, *need* to keep this child. He is an American."

I could not believe what I was hearing—he had not even witnessed me as a mother. It was as if he was reading from a badly memorized script. I couldn't believe it. After more than a year of knowing Lucas, I realized that I had no idea who he was, besides, in my opinion, a liar helping Brian take my child from me. I looked at the judge, who seemed astonished by his remarks, especially since I had not had an opportunity to be a mom to my son yet. She continued to listen while Lucas, the only witness, sat there betraying me and speaking lies that placed an even larger barrier between my son and me.

The next thing I knew, I was being called to the witness stand. I sat in the booth in front of Brian and his lawyer. To prepare for this moment, I had been practicing my English daily since Leonardo's birth.

Speaking to me in a singsong voice, as if I was a toddler, Brian's lawyer said, "Argentina, I am going to ask you a few questions. Is that okay?"

I nodded yes, but the judge told me I had to verbally answer. I said, "Okay."

"Argentina, have you had any children before?" she asked.

I answered proudly, "Yes, a daughter. She is currently back in the Dominican Republic with my family. My wonderful mother is taking care of her while I fix this mess. I was here for training for my job, and I got stuck. My daughter is lovely. Her name is Sabella. We speak every day."

She looked at me harshly. "Just answer the question. I don't need to know her name." She smirked at me and continued, "Argentina, is it true that you haven't seen your daughter in over a year?"

She was trying to intimidate me, but I wasn't letting her.

"Yes," I said. "And I am going to be here for a while, but the next time I see her, it will be to show her a beautiful new baby brother, Leonardo."

"How old is your daughter?"

"She just turned seven."

"And do you know where she is and what she is doing right now?"

I paused and said, "Well, currently she is in an amazing private school in the Dominican learning how to be a smart young lady."

There was no way I was going to let her win. Yes, it had been a very long time since I had seen Sabella. Yes, this was a terrible situation. But I couldn't let the lawyer see my heart breaking on the witness stand. I was too proud.

Brian's lawyer was a tacky woman to me. She spat when she spoke. She may have dressed like a lawyer, but in my eyes, she was far from a classy lady, with her expensive, designer scarf tied tight around her throat, and her women's suit draped ever so heavily around her body. Her grey stilettos seemed to stab the wooden floor with every step, and in my mind, I can still hear the tip-tap of her heels. The whole outfit had no hope of impressing anyone, especially me. I saw it up close every time she spoke to me that day. I could have reached out and touched her if I wanted to. But I didn't want to touch her; rather, I wanted to reach out, grab the scarf, and strangle her with that damn thing until she turned blue. But no matter how hard she tried that day, I refused to let her get away with helping take Leonardo from me. I hadn't seen Sabella in over a year, and I hadn't seen Leonardo in two months. There was no way I was going to allow myself to lose my son and not be able to see my daughter because of this lawyer with a nasty attitude and an ego bigger than the courtroom.

I couldn't help but wonder what the judge was thinking; she may have been puzzled or compassionate, but I don't think she had stopped looking at me from the moment I got on the stand.

The judge knew that she couldn't do much, but when she looked at me, her eyes were filled with sympathy; it was obvious she was hurting for my situation. Once the questioning was over, the decision was made. The judge explained to my lawyer and me that until my visa was updated and I had a way to provide medical coverage for my son, Brian would have physical custody, but I would be granted visitation rights to see Leonardo in Brian's home. I felt like I had been stabbed in the heart. Even though I knew going into the case that it was not in my favor, I had still held out hope that I would get custody of my son. I felt powerless and hopeless.

Though this was far from what I wanted, I was grateful that I would at least be able to see my son again. I looked at the judge. She had a solemn look on her face. She hardly looked back at me. I thought again about her choice of words when she handed down the decision, and then it all clicked.

"Your honor, may I ask a question?" I said.

She told me that I could.

I asked her, "Are you telling me that if I get another visa and obtain health care for my son, I *might* be able to have him back?"

She replied, "That is exactly what I am saying."

I was stunned. There was a way to get Leonardo back.

Court was adjourned, and we all left the courtroom. Even though I could now see him, he was still far from my own child. While I was walking out of the courthouse, I heard Brian and Lucas talking. They were celebrating a seemingly successful court case. And suddenly, I was in pieces once again.

But my dear friend Lemuel held my shattered remains together by holding my hand. He looked me straight in the face and wiped my tears away.

"Argentina, you need your visa in order to get this baby back, do you understand?" he asked slowly.

I nodded in reply.

He told me that there was a way to gain my visa quickly, and it was nearly cost free. He looked me in the eye and squeezed my hand a little harder.

"Will you marry me?" he asked.

I knew he loved me. He had loved me from the day we met. We had talked about it before. He was my friend and my confidant, and we had an amazing bond, but not love. I didn't love him back like that, and I was afraid I never would.

"Would you be okay with that, Argentina?"

Would I? I had no idea.

I told him that I was scared. I was scared for me, my baby, and my future. I was scared for him. I was shocked and dumbfounded by his proposal. As much as I wanted my baby back, the last thing I wanted was to hurt him or our friendship.

So I squeezed his hand the way he squeezed mine, and a tear fell from my eye that he couldn't catch. I loved him like I would love a brother or a friend, nothing more. Yet there we were, barely ten minutes after the hearing, and this caring man had just popped the question. Not exactly what I was expecting.

"But what if I never love you? What then?" I asked quietly.

He looked at the sidewalk and took a breath.

Holding back tears, Lemuel told me that there was more than enough love for the three of us in his heart. I nodded in reply once more. He had his answer.

THE FIGHT CONTINUES

There was a wedding to plan, a dress to find, witnesses to gather, and very, very little time to go home and come back to the city for a wedding to take place. We had to hurry, because I knew Brian would try to pull another fast one. My new fiancé, Lucecita, Harold, and I jumped into Harold's big black Jeep and left the courthouse, speeding directly back to Lucecita and Harold's home to find a dress and to get the necessary paperwork. I hopped out of the car and ran to the front door of their beautiful, spacious house on the outskirts of town. There was no time for tea and no time to sit. We headed straight to her dress closet in the back of the house.

There were more outfits in her closet than I had ever seen anyone own. It was a rainbow—organized by their color, then style, on wooden hangers. The closet was huge, about the size of my bedroom, and every dress was fresh-pressed and dry-cleaned. We searched and searched for the perfect dress for my wedding day. I flew through dozens of styles and labels, all of them untouched, still with department store tags. Then Lucecita grabbed a dress and asked if I liked it.

The dress was beautiful. It was dyed somewhere between navy and royal blue and had grey and white polka dots all over. The sleeves and top of the dress were made of mesh. It was a lighter blue than the rest of the dress, and my skin showed through just a little bit. It still had the store tags attached to it. I loved it. It was unorthodox for a wedding dress, but I suppose that was fitting, considering the unusual circumstances of the wedding.

In the morning, we were off again. We were excited and chatty, and the three hours on the road flew as Lemuel and I headed toward a new future. Our wedding day went by so quickly I can hardly remember it now, but I do remember at the courthouse, Lemuel was excited and looked so well put together in his handsome suit. We were announced as husband and wife, shared a gentle kiss, exchanged big smiles, and the ceremony was over. The day was a blur, but by late afternoon, we were married. And I could not have been more grateful.

As quickly as we had arrived, my new groom and I left. It was eerie going back to where Leonardo was born and still not having him with me. But it didn't matter—I was holding the paper that would prove to immigration that I was no longer just a visitor with a renewable work permit, but a permanent resident. I was married, and I was ready to continue fighting for my child with Lemuel at my side.

We flew down the highway back to town without stopping for anything, straight to the lawyer's office to file a case for the return of Leonardo. I hadn't slept in over a day and a half, but I was more awake than I had ever been.

We walked into the lawyer's office early in the evening, and he looked up from his desk. "I've been waiting for you," he smiled. I took out the certificate and gave it to him. He looked it over, grinned a little, and told me that we finally had a legitimate opportunity to get Leonardo back. I had done the right thing by marrying Lemuel, thank God. With my marriage certificate in hand, I immediately applied for a visa to ensure my stability in America. Since I had legally come here with a work permit, I just had a short waiting period for my Green Card, and I could be reunited with my baby.

During this time of waiting, I visited Leonardo every chance I could get. This was sad and difficult because I was only allowed to see my baby at Brian's house. I constantly worried about Leonardo because of his health conditions, due to being born so prematurely. I longed to be with him permanently so I could truly care for him like a mother should. Whenever I had to leave Leonardo, I cried. There were times I tried to breastfeed him but wasn't producing enough milk because of my stress and anxiety. My emotions were up and down, but I tried to stay focused and do whatever I needed to do to get my baby back.

One evening, I received a phone call from Brian's sister, Tia, who lived in Chicago. Tia said Brian and Vivian had taken Leonardo to Chicago, on the pretext of a visit, without informing the court system or me.

She said, "I just wanted to tell you that Leonardo is here, Argentina. He is beautiful, and I am taking good care of him, okay?"

Her complete honesty and respect took me by surprise. I didn't say much, simply because trust was a short commodity at that point, and I didn't want to say anything that could work against me. However, she told me that she would do everything in her power to help me get my little Leonardo back. I knew that she was very close to Brian, so I did not expect her to help me. I was grateful for her phone call, and it helped me worry a little less knowing where he was.

"He needs his mother," she said firmly, and I could hear the sincerity in her voice.

I was still supposed to be able to see Leonardo, but Brian's visit to Chicago scared me. I felt powerless and alone. What if he stayed in Chicago with Leonardo, and I never got to see him again? I hated the fact that Brian was letting Vivian play mom to my child. Even though I was upset about not seeing my baby and about Brian's latest trick, I knew I had to work on the court case. I thanked Tia and immediately began working with the lawyer, who was helping to prepare me for the case while I stabilized my living situation. I informed my lawyer that Brian had gone to Chicago with Leonardo. This fact benefited my side of the case because I was supposed to be able to visit Leonardo whenever I wanted, and with Brian in Chicago, that was impossible.

After having Leonardo, I had slid into postpartum depression, and I was still struggling, and it did not help that I did not have my son by my side. I was a mix of anxiety and sadness. I felt as if I was walking against the wind. With every step I tried to take forward, I was pushed even further back. It took every ounce of my strength and willpower to even get out of bed in the mornings. Sometimes I wished that I would never wake up. I often had to force myself to shower, brush my teeth, and even eat; I would even sometimes blend up food just to get the nutrients I needed to keep going. I struggled to see a point, and everyday tasks seemed so overwhelming. I became very quiet and did not want to see or talk to anybody. I knew, however, that I had to stay strong and healthy if I ever wanted to get my son back. I had to take it day by day and little by little. I made a schedule to stay focused.

Each day, I would get up, turn on the lights and open the blinds, pray, shower, get dressed, and eat something before I went to see Leonardo. I would go on small walks and listen to music to take my mind off everything and stay away from my bed. I prayed every day because it was in my schedule, but at this point I was angry with God. I constantly questioned, "Why did you take my son?" But no matter how I upset I was with my situation, I followed the schedule anyway. I wanted answers quickly, but God taught me to be patient and rely on Him. Thankfully, my friend Lucecita always remained by my side, then and now. I knew I could trust her, and it was good to have someone to confide in and to talk to. I knew each task I accomplished, no matter how small it seemed, meant I was a step closer to being reunited with Leonardo and obtaining custody of my baby boy.

The final court date was a few weeks after I had returned to town and filed for my right to have Leonardo. During this time, my new husband and I were working day and night on creating an ideal environment for him. Lemuel and I were also preparing a room for Leonardo. On top of hours of work on our home and on my case, I had to prove that I had an income and health insurance, so I went back to work at the grocery store full time. I was so fortunate that they held my position and kept my benefits while I was away for nearly two months.

This time around, my lawyer had a little more faith in our cause. His positive outlook gave me a feeling of hope. For the first time, I felt that my child might be one step closer to coming home to his mother. After regaining a little bit of confidence and feeling a little stronger, I decided that I needed to speak to Brian. I knew he probably had no desire to speak to me and cared little about my situation, but this was not for him. I needed to talk to him for my sake. I called him the day before the trial and kindly asked him to speak with me the next day. He agreed.

I arrived at the courthouse about 10 minutes earlier than I needed to the following day. Brian was there waiting, as I asked him to be. I looked around the courtyard. The place was deserted. For the first time since I told him that I was carrying Leonardo, I was alone with him. I motioned him to come closer, and he did. I began to speak to him so quietly that I could hardly hear myself talking.

"You have put me through so much shit that hell and back seems short. I have no respect for you whatsoever. Before we go in, you need to know that I will do anything to get my child back. I took one of your pistols before I left you, and I will use it on you if you do not give me my child. Do you understand?"

By the look on his face, I knew he didn't believe me, but it still felt good to say. I knew in my heart that I would not go through with it, but at this point I was consumed with anger and fear, and I was tired of fighting. With that, we walked into the courthouse.

The court session began, and Brian was asked for his opening statement. He looked at his lawyer and back at me, and he knew that there was no reason to keep fighting. I had done my homework. The main reason I could not be with Leonardo was because I did not have a stable immigration status, but now I walked into the courtroom with a new power, my visa to stay in America, as well as the ability to provide health insurance for Leonardo. My case was solid, and there was no way he could attain sole custody of Leonardo, according to the court. Either Brian would share custody, or he would be fighting me forever, so he did not contest it. I think Brian also realized the stress and difficulties that come with raising a child, especially because Leonardo still had health difficulties and had to be watched carefully and constantly.

Brian was quiet and looked pensive. The court did not last long; shortly after arriving, the judge ruled that I would get to be reunited with Leonardo and that Brian and I would now share physical and legal custody. My heart was overwhelmed with happiness, and relief filled my soul. There was no more waiting or hoping; I was going to get to be with my son, whom I had been apart from for far too long.

"Court is adjourned," the judge announced.

I had walked in empty-handed but walked out with a court order to get my child back, which explained that I could spend time with my child immediately. After two hospitalizations, a restraining order against me, Brian's surprise trip to Chicago, and incredible amounts of pain, suffering, sadness, and lack of sleep due to anxiety and depression, I had won. He was finally mine.

NUEVA VIDA (NEW LIFE)

Baby Leonardo was at last mine to love and to hold after almost three months of being apart from me. Brian and Vivian were living and working together at this point, and she had been playing mommy to my son for far too long. I couldn't wait another moment. I desperately needed to hold my baby again and get him out of Brian's control. On hearing the judge's words, Lemuel, Lucecita, Harold, and I looked at each other and beamed with excitement. Lemuel and I ran to his car and hopped in. We drove away from the courthouse to Brian's home, with Lucecita and Harold following close behind.

Upon arriving at the house that I used to call home, I jumped out of my seat and onto the snow-covered driveway. I stormed up the few snow-dusted steps to the house and firmly banged on the door. A few seconds passed. I felt Vivian wasn't coming quickly enough, and I was filled with anxiety. I knocked again, but this time I noticed that the door was unlocked, which was not unusual in this small town, but surprising, nonetheless. I barged in.

There he was. Baby Leonardo was lying fast asleep in a car seat on the sofa. Wearing a portable monitor for his sleep apnea, which was caused by his premature lungs at birth, Leonardo was hooked up to a machine sitting next to him on the floor. I took off my scarf and wrapped his head in the warm fabric to shield him from the harsh winter outside. About this time, Vivian came into the room.

"What are you doing here?" she exclaimed.

"I am here to bring my baby home," I replied. "I am his mom." She interrupted me and told me matter-of-factly that I had no right. Then I flashed my papers for her to see, I picked up Leonardo, and we were on our way. She couldn't keep my baby or stop us this time.

On the car ride home, I stared at my tiny baby snuggled in his car seat next to me on the back seat. Lemuel drove to his condominium where Leonardo and I would be living with him. I grabbed the baby carrier and walked up the stairs. Lemuel and I had worked hard to prepare for this day. I was amazed by how much he had done for me, a woman he first encountered at the grocery store. Who would have thought that he would one day be my husband and change my life by helping me to reunite with my son? I guess no one really knows what can happen in life, but that's okay, I decided. It may be a roller coaster, but even with its ups and downs, life's still quite a ride. I loved him and still love him to this day because of his kindness and dedication to a young, round-bellied Dominican woman with a tiny infant. I feel as if he was my personal guardian angel.

Lemuel was a perfect gentleman. He and I slept in separate rooms upon my request. I was still recovering mentally and physically, and we knew that our bond was a deeply caring friendship. Although we kissed playfully, we were never intimate. He occasionally bought things for Leonardo even after I started working. We would sometimes go to the park and enjoy the day. We loved walking together and looking at the leaves, and we would even collect them. Lemuel loved explaining to me facts about the various kinds of trees we would encounter. Whenever I could, I made nice dinners with food that I had shopped for and bought to thank him. It was a good arrangement for us both. He often told me that his condominium seemed dull before I moved in. Now it was alive, he said.

He was always so good with Leonardo. He was so fond of him he began calling him Leo for short. Even though he was Leo's stepfather and had no legal obligations to him, he took the time to play with him and to make him laugh. Though there was no possibility of it being fact, it still felt like Lemuel was his real dad. We were so lucky to have him in our lives.

During this time, Brian had moved to Chicago, but he was still seeing Leonardo. Brian and I kept in contact, and Brian was constantly bringing up the idea of me leaving Lemuel to be with him again instead. I was confused and I didn't know what to do. I didn't want to tell Lemuel because I did not want to hurt him. He had done so much for both Leonardo and I.

About three months into my time with Lemuel, he told me he had met someone. I was overjoyed for him. I told him to bring the girl over for dinner so I could meet her. She was bubbly and sweet, and they had a lot in common, both being engineers. Her name was Clara. I made her pork chops and my grandmother's famous strawberry salad. *Salade para morir (*salad to die for), my grandmother always said, and Clara agreed that it was fabulous. She walked away with the recipe.

I knew that Lemuel loved her from the moment she walked in the door. I knew from the look on his face. I had seen myself in the mirror with that same goofy smile. Lemuel and I had a short talk over tea. He explained that he would like to get the marriage annulled, but he would only do this if it was the right thing for me, and I told him it was. It was then that I let him know that Brian had called recently and had apologized to me. I let Lemuel know that Brian was no longer with Vivian, and he wanted us to be together again and had asked me to move to Chicago with him. I felt sad for Lemuel because I knew he cared for me, but I knew in my heart that I did not love him the way that he deserved to be loved. I never understood why, even though Brian had put me through so much pain, I believed he was the love of my life.

Lemuel and I talked about our dreams for the future. We agreed that this was the best decision for both of us, and that was the end of our short marriage and my safe haven with him. He deserved to be happy, and I wanted to believe I was doing what was best for Leonardo, for me, and even for his dad if we wanted any possibility of being a whole family. I also admitted to Lemuel that being with Brian would allow me to keep an eye on how he was as a parent. Knowing what I went through and how much I worried about my baby's well-being, Lemuel said he understood.

When Brian had called, he told me that he had not been ready to make a commitment before, but he was now. For Leonardo's sake and mine, I wanted to believe him. Brian also told me he would help me get an immigration lawyer to make sure that my immigration status remained stable. He had sold his restaurant in the mountains out West and had relocated to Chicago to start a new career.

Even though I was still angry and a little afraid for the future, and even though I was astonished that Brian (or anyone for that matter) could have done such a terrible thing, I knew that Leonardo tied Brian and me together. He was his dad, and he had a right to raise him alongside me because of this connection. He also said he would keep his promise of bringing my daughter Sabella back to me here in the States so we could be a family. The stability of a real family life was the option he offered, and this was what I had wanted for us when I first let him know I was pregnant. All I had ever wanted was to be a happy family together, so despite my concerns about trusting him, I said yes to his proposal.

Brian drove from Chicago to pick up Leonardo and me from the mountain town I had called home for a while. One last time, Lemuel kissed Leonardo on the forehead and told him, with a smile, that it was nice to know him. He looked sad, like he was holding back tears. He had raised him like a son for three months, after all. I put Leo in the car seat and looked at my savior. Lemuel didn't say anything to me, so I waved goodbye to him and got in the SUV, and we drove off. Lemuel went back to his condominium and watched from his window as we drove away. His image faded as our distance grew. I didn't thank him again, and it's one of my biggest regrets. But I don't even think "thank you" would have been the right words or enough. What he did for us meant so much more than that.

On our trip to Chicago, it was apparent that Brian and I still had feelings for each other, and we talked about our new life together and about a new job offer that he had received in another state. He seemed happy to see us, and it made me feel good to see how loving he was toward Leonardo. He was always talking to him and carrying him in and out of the truck when we stopped. Along the way, I was kept wondering what I was doing, but I knew I was happy to see him. When we were driving to Chicago, he asked me to marry him, and I was stunned because I had waited a long time to hear those words. In my mind, I felt marrying Brian would be the easiest thing to do. I knew in my heart that I wasn't over Brian yet; he was my first love and the father of my son. When I had dated Bruno I was very young, and while he was the father of my first child, most of our relationship was an escape for me, but Brian was the first guy I felt a deep connection with. After pausing quietly to think for a few minutes, I replied, "Yes, I will marry you, but we will have to wait."

I reminded him we still had to go through the process of annulling my marriage with Lemuel, and we needed to take it step by step. I also told him that I wanted to take a trip home to visit my family and my daughter and introduce them to Leonardo, and when I returned, I would be ready to marry him. He told me he would give me all the time I needed and that we would work on everything together. We talked about our plans the entire way to Chicago.

During the trip, we shared a lot of tears for what had happened, along with kisses for forgiveness, and I felt that this time Brian did indeed love me back and that he truly cared and was ready to make a real commitment to Leonardo and me.

He told me, "We are going to be a family. I wasn't ready before, but I am now."

A New Home for Us

When we got to Chicago, I saw where I was going to live. It was a temporary home for us, considering that we were planning to move very soon, but it was beautiful. I finally got to see Brian's sister Tia again and thank her in person for the phone call she had made and for the support she had given me. She told me that she had no idea why Brian acted the way he did, and she added Leonardo's *abuela* (Brian's mom) was very disappointed. "You never take a child from its mother," she said.

We stayed in Chicago until Leonardo was eight months old. After nights of worrying and trying to find the correct words, I placed a phone call to my family in the Dominican Republic and told my mother and my brother Poli that they had a new little family member. I had spoken to my family often, especially to talk to Sabella, but I had not told them about the pregnancy or everything that had happened. The response was better than I expected. I was afraid that they would be harsh with me, but instead, they told me to come home, and they would ask questions then. I explained about the issues in court that I had dealt with, and how I lost custody of Leonardo for so long to Brian. When I asked if Brian could come with me to visit them, the answer was a firm, "No, not yet."

They didn't trust him enough (and rightfully so, considering what had happened). Brian let me go with little fuss, and it made me think maybe I could trust him a little more than I could after the entire fiasco surrounding Leonardo's birth. I was so excited to see my family for the first time in almost two years. More than anything, I was so excited to see my Sabella and even more excited to let her meet her new baby brother.

When we arrived at the airport I quickly realized the secret was out—we were met by everyone, including my parents and my siblings, which was a little overwhelming, but I wouldn't have had it any other way. We exchanged innumerable hugs and kisses to make up for almost two years of absence. Everyone was talking at once; they were so excited to see us and to meet Leonardo for the first time.

After missing her so much and for so long, I finally got to see my daughter, who was so happy to see me. Sabella had long braids and was wearing a white dress. Since I had last seen her, she had grown so much and had so many questions about her little brother and me. She loved her baby brother's green eyes and blonde hair. It was nice to have Sabella and Leonardo together for the first time. Sabella was thrilled to meet her little brother. She was always smart and inquisitive, and as excited as I was to see her, after the long trip home, I was having trouble focusing on her nonstop questions. Once I had a little rest and some time with my family, I spent most of my time with Sabella; we talked about America and how excited I was to bring her there.

Shortly after arriving, I decided to go and visit my Uncle Pablo on his farm. It had been a long time since I had been to his farm, and stepping foot on the soil immediately brought back memories of when we would visit in my childhood. It felt freeing to be back at the place that had been my escape while I was growing up. I loved watching Sabella play with Leonardo, and Leo was fascinated by the chickens. My uncle Pablo always seemed to bring a smile to my face and make me feel at peace. I think it was because of his calm demeanor. He never seemed stressed, and I had never witnessed him angry. I was so excited to see him again.

One afternoon, when the children were taking a nap, my brother Poli asked me to sit on the patio, and he went inside and got a pitcher of lemonade and two glasses. When he came back outside, he sat down beside me and questioned me about my time in America. My brother Poli was now a lawyer, and I held nothing back about my issues with its policies, like what happened with almost losing Leonardo because of Brian's legal maneuvering. I began to unfold the story of going to court to obtain custody of Leonardo and the pain I went through fighting for my baby.

"I wish you would have been there to witness everything," I explained to my older brother. "I felt like my hands were tied. Because I didn't have an active visa at the time, I could not have my son. When I originally went to America, I did not expect it to turn out like this."

Poli looked at me with compassion and explained kindly, "I don't want you to feel bad, but I think I am the right person to tell you. Even though I do not have a perfect understanding of the law in U.S., I think the judge did not have many choices, based on Leonardo's health conditions and the problems with your visa."

I broke in, "So it wasn't enough that I was his mother?"

He nodded his head in agreement and said, "I think that everything was based on your status. I know it sucks. But you fought hard, and now you have Leonardo. He is very lucky to have a mother like you, who loves him so much." He continued, "I know you are enjoying being back here in the Dominican, but you can't stay here forever. You know you have to go back to the U.S."

In my heart, I knew Poli was right. I had to return to America. I told Poli, "Brian wants to marry me. He told me that he is going to change and will prove to me that we can be a family. He is going to help me bring Sabella to America because he knows it has been my dream to have a family and to have Sabella and Leonardo together." I added, "I want to believe him, but it is so hard to trust him. Sometimes I look at Brian and I love him, but other times I cannot stand to see his face for what he did."

Poli told me, "I understand that, but people make mistakes. Maybe he wasn't thinking right at the time you got pregnant, and maybe he wasn't ready to have a relationship or be a father." He pointed out, "It could be that after he saw his son, he had a change of heart. I know he hurt you very much, but I think you should give him a chance to be a father and a husband. I also think it is smart for you to marry him, since he is willing to help you stabilize your status and bring Sabella to America."

Poli stood up and hugged me. "I am so proud of you, *manita* [little sister]" he said. "You are so strong, and I love you. You are also a wonderful mother to Sabella and Leonardo."

I felt a little better about the situation I was in. It was so good to have my brother to talk to once again.

Shortly after I arrived, I talked with my father, and I'm not going to lie, I was still bitter about his issues with alcoholism, abuse, and infidelity, but he was still my dad. He wanted to talk to me about the baby and said he wanted to keep us safe, so I told him everything, from start to finish. A few hours into our conversation, I noticed a familiar look on his face. He was thinking, and since he always had a plan, I knew that he was trying to create another one for me right then. Even though we had major differences, we still had our determination in common. He paused the conversation and then asked me if I had Leonardo's birth certificate and my visa.

I responded, "Yes, I do."

He then asked me, "Do you want to keep Brian from being able to take Leonardo again?"

Naturally, I responded, "Yes." Secretly, I was still terrified that Brian would take him again.

My dad told me to go and get the birth certificate and my visa and bring them to him. When I returned, I handed him the papers. To my tremendous surprise, he got out his lighter and set the papers afire. He looked at me and said, "Now he can't possibly get Leo out of this country on his own, at least not for a while. Do you have a letter that allows you to take Leonardo out of the country?"

Uncertain of what was going on and a little unsure of how to respond, I told him that I did, and he told me to keep the letter in a safe place. At this point, I couldn't believe what he had done and thought that this was probably a combination of one of the craziest and most brilliant ideas, because it meant that Brian couldn't take Leo out of my home country, at least not for a while. It was a very strange thing for my dad to do for me, I thought, but in his own controlling way, he was trying to protect me and his grandson. For now, at least we were safe at home in the Dominican Republic. I was okay. I was with my family—my brothers, my sisters, my mom, and both of my children. I felt at ease for the first time in a long time.

Even though my father and I had our differences, his extreme precautions for our safety demonstrated that he did care about me. He was far from the perfect father, but I realized he was willing to protect my son and me. He had proven his love in his own way, and I felt a little more at peace with him.

BACK TO AMERICA

Brian was not very happy about having to work so hard to get us back to the States, which took almost two months, but he did it. He went through the trouble of hiring a lawyer and filling out an immense amount of paperwork just to get us back. While I was in the Dominican Republic, there were a lot of phone calls back and forth between Brian and me as we tried to sort out the situation, and we began to reconnect. He was willing to do so much for me and Leonardo, and he was going out of his way to prove he wanted us to be together. I finally felt sure that getting back together with him was the right thing to do, and I could tell that he was serious when he kept asking me to marry him. Brian knew all the right things to say and do to make me trust him again, and I was excited to return to the U.S. and start the process of filling out paperwork so that Sabella could finally join us once I obtained my permanent visa.

I finally felt like I had the chance to have a family that was stable and healthy. Shortly after I returned from the Dominican Republic, we moved to Mississippi for Brian's job. We tried to be happy, and for a while, our lives were going well. Brian worked during the day, and I began working at a restaurant at night while Brian watched Leonardo. Eventually, we went to the courthouse and got married.

Sabella was still living with my parents, and her father visited her regularly at their home. Unfortunately, while I was working on her paperwork, Sabella's father, Bruno, snatched her from my parents' home on one of his visits. My friend Perla called me one day completely shocked that Bruno would do such a thing. None of us saw this coming, and we desperately tried to figure out how to find her and get her back. Bruno had told my parents he was taking Sabella to lunch, but instead, he took her with him to live where he had relocated, and he didn't tell anyone where that was.

I was so worried. I knew that Bruno was a good father and he was taking care of Sabella, but I could not believe that he had the nerve to take off with her. To say I was upset was an understatement. I was so close to being finished with the paperwork so Sabella could move to the States with me, and now there was a new obstacle. But like with every other near-impossible challenge, I decided I would do whatever it took to find Sabella and bring her to live with us.

I was frantic trying to find where they had gone. We had to start from nothing in order to find my daughter. Brian and I hired a private investigator to help us search for her. At first I thought she was in Puerto Rico, because Bruno had been living there, but we discovered Bruno was now living in Texas. We began calling every school in the state, searching for my daughter. After 30 days, we finally tracked Sabella down. Those 30 days of anxiety and worry felt like years to me. I hated not knowing where my daughter was and not being able to talk to her. We found her in one of the schools and arranged for police to accompany us as we went to pick her up. Sabella was very confused by the entire situation.

I stayed in Texas for several weeks negotiating with her father over a custody arrangement. We eventually agreed to share custody. She would spend part of her time with him in Texas and the rest of the time with us. I asked Brian to find a job in Texas to make it easier for Sabella's father and me to share custody. I did not want Sabella to have to travel back and forth; I wanted her to be able to remain in the same school she had been attending. I did not want to put her through another transition.

It was around this time I became pregnant with Victoria, *mi princesa* (my princess). Victoria was totally planned. I had wanted another daughter for years and years, and I wanted at least two of my children to have the same father and be together. Knowing this, Brian tried his best to make me happy. He promised that he would try and work on correcting his flaws like making fun of my accent, and he did not disappoint me. I had come full circle; I was back in a place in America I had first called home when I was training as a flight attendant.

As planned, Victoria was our Christmas baby. When she was born, she was eight pounds. She had light skin, brown hair, and big brown eyes. For her first Christmas, she was in the bassinet next to the tree in a little red dress with a flower in her hair.

It was hard for Sabella and me to let her go to sleep, because we both loved her so much and hated having to be separated from her, even though I reminded myself and Sabella that it was necessary for Victoria to get her rest. We would often sing her to sleep. Whenever she was awake, I held her and basked in the sheer joy of holding my beautiful newborn baby. Victoria was my first baby that I didn't have to leave, so I was overprotective and refused to let her out of my sight. She was a very happy baby. Her first word was *pajarito* (bird), which was uncommon for a first word, but nevertheless, very entertaining to her family. She would call every animal she saw pajarito; it was adorable. Victoria was a friendly and sweet child, and I enjoyed getting to watch her grow up. Sabella and Leonardo loved having a little sister. It was one of the happiest times of my life—I had Sabella, Leonardo, and Victoria together. We were a complete family, at last. At that moment, my life seemed perfect.

Then Brian lost his job in Texas, and we eventually transferred to St. Louis for Brian's new job, where he worked as a leading manager for a company that owned many chains of restaurants, so he had to travel frequently. Sabella was now old enough to decide where she wanted to live, and she chose to stay in Texas. It would have been difficult for her to move so far away from her friends and her life in Texas, even though I longed to have her with us permanently. However, we always made sure Sabella came to visit us in St. Louis at least once a month.

Even though Brian had promised to work on our happiness together, my memories of his taking Leonardo proved to be too much, and his unpredictability didn't help. It was difficult moving so often, this time to St. Louis, which was not easy and made me feel insecure again because I had to completely start over finding friends and a new job—not to mention the constantly shifting St. Louis weather, which drove me crazy.

A year or so after we were married, Brian's character became clearer to me, and I started to realize that we had fallen in love so quickly that we didn't really know each other. I found that my inability to trust him made me feel uneasy and insecure, and his restlessness, like the weather, bothered me a lot. Brian was constantly on the move: changing jobs, changing his address, or changing his mind. He was also traveling a lot with his job and rarely home. When he was home, he would be loving one day, but the next day, he would be remote. Fortunately, he didn't drink, but he did like to be in control.

The worst part was the times Brian and I would get into an argument and he would make comments that the kids were his and because I was not a citizen of the United States yet, he could take my children away. We argued often because Brian was constantly coming and going. He would often not tell me when he was going out of town. He quickly became very controlling in our relationship, and I did not know how to deal with it, but I knew I needed to stand up for myself and my children. I can remember him discussing that if we ever got divorced, he would take Leonardo and leave Victoria with me. I could not bear the thought of separating my children or being apart from either of them. I had walked through years of being apart from my children, and I was not going to allow it to happen again. Being a mother to my children was the greatest reward, and I refused to have that snatched from me. I was haunted by the possibility that he could do something like that again. Even if he was not entirely serious with his threats, they played with my emotions, causing them to be up and down, which made me feel constantly upset and worried. The anxiety from the frequent separations and my fear about what he had done in the past became too much. Even though I tried, his ongoing threats of taking Leonardo meant I could no longer trust Brian.

Three years after Victoria's birth, the marriage fell apart. It was obvious he wanted to move on, and I no longer wanted to deal with his erratic behavior. For a while, we battled about the specifics of the divorce, especially about the custody of the kids.

In the end, the divorce seemed to go smoothly. Brian and I agreed to share custody of the children, and he was ordered to pay child support. That went okay until he married again not too long after the divorce. Shortly thereafter, he took me back to court to reduce child support. In court, it seemed to me like Brian's intention was to split the kids up so he did not have to pay the full amount. Once again, I had to prove that I could raise my children, and on my own. Brian argued that he had a stable life and was now remarried.

It was a stressful time for me, thinking about going back to court once again and fearing the idea of Brian obtaining sole custody of my children. But I had some winning evidence on my side.

I would commonly receive calls from Brian asking me to pick up the kids after school or after practice or even a game because he wasn't able to pick them up in time. It was alarming to find Leonardo or Victoria, who were so little, to be the last child after an event waiting to be picked up. I tried to hide how upset I was from them, and not to let on that their dad had forgotten them, but I also realized I couldn't count on Brian, and they should never have to be waiting by themselves outside an empty building ever again. I took charge of the situation by waiting outside with the kids when Brian was scheduled to pick them up. If he showed up, I would tell them to have fun and send them on their way. If he didn't show up, I would simply say, "Okay, time to go," and act like it was no big deal so they wouldn't feel let down, and so I didn't make him mad or make him look bad in their eyes.

Brian convinced the court to reduce the amount he had to pay in child support, but thankfully, because he was undependable when it was his turn to pick them up from school, he was not successful in obtaining full custody.

While Brian and I may have fallen out of love and have talked only when necessary, he has remained in the picture for Leonardo and Victoria. To them, he is a great dad. Even if we disagreed when the kids were growing up, Brian and I strived to be diplomatic for their sake.

On Our Own

Following my divorce with Brian, I ended up staying in St. Louis long-term. I had no way of moving, so I decided I would make St. Louis our home. When we had first moved to St. Louis, I had taken a job in a restaurant at a local casino. After the divorce, to support myself and my kids, I continued working there as a server while a young lady from Columbia took care of my Leonardo and Victoria. My English was not perfect, but it had come a long way since I first moved to the U.S. While I was working at the casino, I began taking classes at the community college to further my language skills.

After working for a while, I was doing well at my job and decided to ask the casino managers if I could be trained in the other restaurants within the casino, and they happily agreed. They knew that I worked hard, and I needed a more flexible schedule to be with my kids, which training in other restaurants would allow. Knowing so much about my place of work made me valuable to them, and after training in the other restaurants, they promoted me to a leader position. My new work hours allowed me to spend more time with my kids. I was grateful because I was also able to spend more time with Sabella when she came to visit. This schedule worked well for us, so during this time, I attended English classes part-time at the community college. Even though working and taking classes was difficult, and sometimes I felt like I rarely had a break, I knew learning the language would be worth it someday. I knew that getting an education was important so that I would be able to offer my kids a better life.

While I attended classes, the kids would come with me to the community college and stay in childcare there. Some of the best conversations I ever had with my children were while driving there. The entire way, we would listen to music, talk, and laugh, and the kids would eat their favorite snacks. They would sometimes ask, "Why are we going to school again?" and I would answer, "Because mommy needs a better job, and you can do your homework while you're there." I loved this time I would get to spend with them, and it brought us closer together.

Eventually, I quit working for the casino to get away from the cigarette smoke and because I wanted to find a job where I was more in control of my schedule. To do this, I had been saving up money to open my own business. It was time to move on. I had fond memories of my time there because of the staff and the management, but I had other plans for myself and my family, and I wanted to see how far my goals to improve myself and our situation would take me.

Before long, I finally obtained my American citizenship. The process was not easy and took a lot of hard work and dedication, but it was also very exciting. To me, it was informative and fun to learn about the history of America. I felt smart knowing so many facts about America. I learned things that I will be able to use forever. Although the test was intimidating because it was so serious, the excitement of becoming a citizen gave me the motivation to study extra hard. It took a couple of months, but I felt free and happy when I finished. My children were at the ceremony, and I was so excited by what citizenship meant. It felt like an accomplishment that I had come this far. When I sang the national anthem during the ceremony, I cried tears of happiness. From a young age, I had dreamed of becoming an American citizen, and now I had finally made that dream a reality.

With what I had earned and with the experience I had gained at the casino, along with my improving English, I took a big step and started a cleaning business. I needed the flexibility to be home every night with my kids, and this was a great way to accomplish what I needed. I ran the whole business from home. Surprisingly, it didn't take too long before the business was doing well. I realized then that I had learned a lot of my business skills from my father. Considering how much anxiety he had caused me, it wasn't easy to admit how much he had taught me, including setting up a proper business plan, staying organized, and buying newspaper and magazine ads. My father's legacy was both my curse and my inspiration.

Around this time, my father's health started to decline quickly. He was diabetic and still drinking, which was making his condition worse. He needed to have his leg amputated, but his machismo made him too stubborn. He refused even when the doctors told him he would die without the surgery. I flew to the Dominican Republic to see him in his last days and to help my mom care for him. He was only 65, but he was dying, and I felt helpless. We talked, and I read to him, and we both apologized to each other because of how often we disagreed in the past. I felt sorry for him when I knew it was the end. After a lifetime of alcohol-based behavior, he was sick, he was sober, and he was nice. I sat by his side and held his hand. I finally got to tell him, "I wish this would have been different, so our family wouldn't have grown up with so much anxiety and anger, but I have and will forever love you."

While my father was in the hospital, my Uncle Pablo visited him frequently. He was always there making sure that he was comfortable and well cared for. Before he died, my uncle and I asked if he had repented, and he said, "Yes." We all cried. He didn't often go to church toward the end, but I asked him if he wanted a pastor, and he said, "Yes." My uncle and I could see how peaceful he looked after he had repented, and we could see that he was no longer angry.

He died three days later. While he was in the hospital, I refused to leave his side. He was loving at the end. Having this time together with my dad was precious because I was able to tell him that it wasn't all bad, that I had learned a lot from him, and that I wasn't mad at him. Regardless of the things that happened between us, having this last conversation helped me to gain closure and to forgive him.

When he was sick, my mom had done what she needed to do and was always charitable to him. He had cut his own life short. She cried when he died but has since found contentment on her own. Mom decided to keep the one grocery store closest to her house and sell the rest. For the first time, my mother was on her own and could relax.

My mother is happy now, surrounded by her kids, grandkids, and friends in the Dominican Republic. She travels to the U.S. to visit me. When she visits St. Louis, she loves going to baseball games and to the mall to go shopping. I have never met someone stronger than my mom. She is a fighter and an incredible woman. All her children are doing well and have remained close. She has done what she had told her kids to do: "No matter what, keep going."

RICHARD IN CHARGE

By the time I was in my thirties, I was no longer married, but my kids and I were doing okay. It had been about five years since Brian and I divorced. I had a successful cleaning business, and our lifestyle was stable. We had a nice condominium in a good school district in St. Louis. We were on our own, and it felt good to be independent and doing well.

One day, I received a phone call to go to meet with a new prospective client to give him a quote to clean his house. I was prepared to have Richard become my client. Yet when we met, Richard made it clear he had other plans as he showed me around his big, elegant, professionally decorated home. There he was, this older gentleman around 60, with a beautiful house and a flirtatious attitude. He was very polite and kept asking me if I wanted anything to drink, which I declined. But after I quoted him the price for cleaning his home, he asked me on a date. I responded by saying that I do not date clients, so he smiled and immediately fired me, then asked me out again. A couple of days later, we went out on a date. He picked me up and took me to a nice dinner. We talked for hours and had a wonderful time. I had been working hard and taking care of my kids, so it felt nice to go out. I quickly fell for him. I decided to keep him as a client, which at the time seemed like a good idea.

It felt good to go out to dinner and have some fun after spending a long time focused only on work and my children. Shortly after we started dating, I introduced Richard to my children, who showed an immediate discomfort and said they didn't like him. Upon asking them what the issue was, they said that they just had a bad feeling about him. One mistake I made was introducing Richard to my kids too soon, and the other was not really listening to them. Unfortunately for them and for me, I ignored their complaint and continued to date him.

During this time, Brian once again told me he would like to split the children up. He told me because Leonardo was a boy, he needed to be with his father. He also said it would make it easier on me if I didn't have both Leonardo and Victoria to take care of. I was so angry and disappointed because I had worked so hard to be where I was. I loved both Leonardo and Victoria dearly, and I refused to separate them. I knew I was strong enough to raise my children together. I was already struggling with only being able to have Sabella part-time, and I knew that splitting up the other children would only increase my anxiety. It was so stressful having the kids visit him because he always wanted to keep Leonardo.

I said to Brian, "Why is it that whenever I am on my feet, you want to push me down? What's your problem? You know that I am not going to let you split the kids; they need to be together. Follow the court order and pick them up when you are supposed to pick them up. I am tired of having this same conversation. Do your part, and I will do mine."

I was becoming very uneasy not knowing what Brian would do. My fears about the children motivated me to lean towards Richard because I needed someone to protect us, and Richard had the means to do it. The kids eventually grew fond of Richard; he was going out of his way to be nice to them and would frequently buy them presents. When he asked me to marry him after a year of dating, I agreed.

Richard wanted to purchase a new vacation home in Costa Rica, so after acquiring the house, he decided to hold the wedding there on the property. I would have loved to get married in the Dominican Republic with my entire family there to witness the special occasion, but Richard was set on tying the knot on his terms and on his property. He did, however, fly my children, mother, and sister in for the ceremony. Then, right before the wedding ceremony, Richard handed me a tremendous amount of papers to read and said I had to sign them within the hour. I was stunned by his request and asked him if he could read and explain them to me, but he said the papers just said that he would give me a great life, so I naively signed them.

The ceremony was long and extremely involved, with the surprise addition of the complicated prenuptial agreement he had me sign. I stood by myself and signed the document Richard gave me without properly understanding the papers and without a lawyer. I was so excited to be getting married again, this time to someone with maturity who seemed to command respect, that I ignored signs that I should have paid attention to. In the frenzy of planning, having my hair and makeup done, as well as my mom and sister joining me for the event, I did what felt best and easiest, without asking any questions, which was signing my name on the line. I had confidence in Richard and believed that the agreement was for my own good. My mother and sister, however, felt the same as my children had: Richard was bad news.

My mother, at one point, said "*Mi hijita* [my daughter], what did you just sign?"

My answer was simple: "I don't know."

She then shook her head and told me, "You have given him the right to throw you out at any time. If you're not working and the marriage doesn't work out, what are you going to do for money?"

Embarrassed and upset at the possibility I had just made a big mistake, I snapped back, "He would not do that!"

I fell captive to the lie that I needed a man to protect me and love me to be happy. At the time, I truly thought that Richard was the one—or at least I let myself believe that. Because he was older and seemed so sure of himself, I thought he was ready to settle down; I know I was. After our wedding, Richard completely changed; it was a night-and-day difference. While we had been dating, he would often come over to my house for dinner, and he would take me out to dinner a couple times a week. He was charming to me and treated me well. Shortly after we got married, Richard took me to a fancy restaurant in St. Louis where he was a regular. Right before we walked in, I was surprised, then offended, when he said condescendingly, "Don't worry, you are probably going to get some strange looks because the only Hispanic people who come here are the cleaning people." I was shocked and horrified that Richard would have the nerve to say that to me. He made me feel both embarrassed and insignificant for the rest of the night.

Then my mother's instincts soon proved to be correct, and the unfortunate truth of Richard's nature unfolded when we went on vacation in the Rockies over Christmas not long after the wedding. That's when I started to find out who my new husband really was. It was late in the evening, the kids were in bed, and we were out celebrating life, and Sabella was watching Leonardo and Victoria. I soon grew tired and asked if we could return to "his" vacation home to go to bed. He told me that he would stay, but I could leave. I left, but I was suspicious, considering the number of women who were hanging around him at the restaurant bar in the resort area where we were staying. I knew we had both had too many drinks and we needed to get back home. I hated the fact that Richard stayed and continued to purchase drinks for the women there. I felt, and should have known then, that he had no respect for me at all or we would have left together as a married couple.

I took a taxi back to the house, but then I realized he had the house key. When I got to the house, I noticed the lights were off, so I banged on the door trying to get in by waking up one of the kids. It was below zero, and nobody woke up, despite my persistent, loud knocking. I was freezing—and discouraged that I couldn't get inside late at night in a strange town—so I went to the 24-hour gas station across the street to keep warm. I was watching the road in front of the house through the gas station window, and as soon as I saw Richard drive down the street, I walked back to the house and was standing out front when he returned. I told him that I had no way in. He got angry. He was drunk and slurring his words and said he was mad at me for leaving him early. He grabbed my arm and yanked hard, sending a piercing pain through my arm. He threw me on the floor and told me that I should have banged on the door harder or found another way to get into the house. He was really hurting me, and despite the intense pain in my arm, I tried to defend myself. I tried to kick him to keep him from hurting me worse, but I could only manage to break his glasses. Thankfully, the noise woke the neighbors, and they immediately called the police. They took me to the hospital and hauled him away in handcuffs to jail, where he stayed for nearly two days.

While spending most of the night in the emergency room, I worried about what would happen. After hours of waiting, I was finally seen by the doctor and discovered that my arm was in fact broken. I decided to keep quiet about the incident and not tell my family or friends because I was both embarrassed and afraid.

I asked the police for a ride home when I was released, since I had no money or credit cards or a way to return to my children at Richard's vacation home. I learned on the way home that the police were not really fans of Richard. They gave me the impression that he was a somewhat shady character, and they suggested he had hurt his ex-wife as well.

Looking back on it now, I know I should have just left him then, but I had no means to leave. I had three kids, no access to money on my own, a badly broken arm, and no transportation to return home. It was distressing to realize how quickly my independence had disappeared after I married Richard. When he got out of jail, he was mad at first and said my kids and I could walk home to St. Louis, but in the end, we rode home together with him driving. He was mostly quiet but would occasionally ask me if I had taken my pain medication and if I was feeling better. For safety's sake and to keep peace, I went along with his act, but I remained cautious. Sabella was old enough to know what was going on and privately urged me to leave him.

In my heart, I knew she was right, but I didn't listen to her or to my own questions about his behavior. Instead, I mistakenly thought that having someone I had thought I loved, who could be a father to my kids, meant we were now a family. I was wrong—it didn't. What I didn't truly realize was the bond created by honesty, care, respect, and trust people have for each other makes a family. From that point on, Richard was never, ever family to me because of what he did—and continued to do—during our marriage, because of his abusive behavior to me, and because of what I considered to be manipulation of my children and me. Yet I stayed, because I was too afraid to leave him or to speak up.

My independence slipped away day by day. He took control of me and wouldn't let me work unless it was to help his business. He expected me to stay home and tend to him and the house. I could not escape from his control because he worked from home. I was required to be there to make him breakfast, lunch, and dinner every single day. In exchange for remaining home all day, caring for the house, and helping him with his business, Richard told me he would pay for everything I needed.

At the time I thought this was a good idea because at least it meant I would get to be home with my kids and see them more often. Unfortunately, he also became controlling about the time I spent with my children. He would not let me take them to school and instead would force them to take the bus. I frequently became bored being at home day in and day out. I once asked Richard if I could volunteer somewhere, and he declined my request. I felt trapped and longed for a glimpse of freedom. He even prevented me from going to church, but I still went when he traveled. What got me through all this was keeping the faith and not letting him make me feel worthless. I kept thinking, "It's going to get better tomorrow."

He sold my car, then gave me a fancy new car in his name, which he presented to me like it was mine. Unfortunately, whenever he didn't get his way, he would take away the keys, the money I had for emergencies, and my only credit card, which was a copy of his own. At any moment, he had the ability to rip away everything I owned, which was a very scary and intimidating reality to live in, and he reminded me of that fact whenever he was mad.

When Richard was angry, he would demand I go stay in the bedroom. Then he would close the door and position his big, noisy, dog outside it. The dog would bark loudly to alert him if I tried to leave. Richard always made sure this intimidation happened while the kids were at school, so they had no idea of the mistreatment that was going on. I was living in a constant state of abuse and fear of him, but I tried to keep everything calm for my kids.

Richard would give me presents and then abruptly take them back when he was upset. I wasn't allowed to decorate the house; only he had that privilege. The house was beautiful from the outside, but it was hell on the inside. Richard was very possessive—he didn't want me to go to school and refused to let me have any of my friends over unless it was on his terms. I only managed to keep in touch with some of them through secret connections and by communicating honestly with them about what was going on at home. During this time, Perla was my saving grace. She was always available to listen, no matter what hour of the day it was. She often urged me to leave Richard, but I knew there was no way I could. For the sake of providing for my children, I felt like I had no other choice than to stay.

At home, I suffered and suffered alone because I did not want my kids to be without a family and place to call home. I wish I could have realized then that the only family they needed was each other and myself. Richard was never close to us, because his behavior kept him distant, so there was clearly no emotional benefit to having him in our lives. But at this point, we were dependent on the illusion of financial security, and I kept hoping it was still possible to make the marriage work. Closing my eyes to the abuse my mother had gone through with my father, I kept thinking that because it was so early in my relationship with Richard, maybe we had time to fix it. But my wishful thoughts were very unrealistic.

Depression and anxiety soon became my reality, and I began drinking too much. When Richard and I were first dating, I had started drinking with him when we would go out. He would constantly take me out to fancy restaurants and order bottles of wine, which seemed fun and harmless at the time. However, after getting married, I began to drink quite a bit, even though I had sworn that I would never let alcohol take control of me like it had controlled my dad for so many years. I had grown up around alcohol and had seen the devastating effects it had on my father and my family, but as my home situation grew worse, my good judgment started to slip. There was always alcohol around Richard's house, and anytime I was bored, sad, or feeling isolated, which was often, I would drink. Sadly, I was falling into the same trap of turning to alcohol that my father had sunken into years before. While I did not have the same angry personality he did, it became obvious I needed to make a change as I became more depressed and the marriage became more oppressive.

ENOUGH IS ENOUGH

Eventually, I came to realize that my only hope for being truly happy was to get out of this marriage. I began to do everything I could think of to save up money so my children and I could afford to break free from Richard's control. I would go to the grocery store and purchase gift cards and hide them, so when we left, we could afford groceries. I would purchase items only to return them in order to get the cash back. I collected every piece of change I could find lying around the house. On the rare occasion Richard was in a good mood, I would ask him for a little bit of cash and then secretly save it instead of spending it. This was a very scary time for me. I had seen how terrible Richard's anger was when he got mad in small situations and feared how he would react if he discovered what I was doing. I had to be extremely careful so that he would not find out.

I also knew that I was taking a big chance because Richard was very good at being secretive. After we married, I learned there were a lot of things about his life and past he hid from me. He would lock many of the rooms in his house, including his office, which was always locked. If I wanted to talk to him when he was in his office, he would make me knock on the door before I could enter.

On top of the abuse and the secretiveness, I discovered troubling information about Richard from a woman who identified herself as one of his ex-wives. She contacted me and sent me pictures of women that she said were Richard's "call girls." I was shocked when I saw how many women were in the pictures. I had no idea. I began to consider the red flags that I should have seen earlier in our marriage, and everything began to fall into place.

Her call made me think about how Richard would often pressure me to watch adult films, and I would give in when he made me feel that I had no other choice. I felt like I had to keep silent and do what he asked of me so he would not become angry. He made me feel very uncomfortable and insecure. For one of his birthdays, he told me he wanted a calendar with sexy pictures of me and he hired someone to make it. Until this day, I still do not know what happened to that calendar, which worries me. I also remembered how often Richard liked to surround himself with young women, even when I was around. I was worried about everything his ex-wife told me, especially about the possibility of catching a sexually transmitted disease, which she said he was being treated for, which he denied when I confronted him. When I found pills mixed in with others in our medicine cabinet that proved he had been treated, I questioned him about his past, and he told me that our relationship was different than the ones he had had before, and I believed him.

Then, one night, I overheard him on a suggestive phone conversation with a woman, and it was apparent she was one of the women he spent time with, and this one was recent. Richard told her how wonderful she was the previous night and asked her to come back two nights later for drinks and dinner, "all expenses paid and at double the usual rate." Shocked and disgusted by what this meant—that he *was* hiring call girls—I confronted him. I told him I had heard his conversation, so there was no point in denying it.

After I confronted Richard, he began to cut me off from him. He was sure that I would be afraid because I had no life outside of him, or so he thought. However, even though I was afraid, and even though it was risky, I did have enough courage and foresight to see a lawyer. I was able to ask the lawyer to interpret the papers I had signed at my wedding, and the lawyer explained to me that I would get a little bit of money from Richard for each year I was married to him.

Shortly after talking to the lawyer, I used Richard's credit card and filed for divorce. I was tired of feeling constantly humiliated and trapped by Richard, and I wanted to file first to prove to him and to myself that I could be strong and independent once again. After having a lawyer look over the prenuptial agreement I had previously signed, I found out Richard claimed that if the marriage did not work out, he would help to provide a place for my children and me to live. I knew, however, that Richard assumed I did not completely understand the agreement I had signed since he had only quickly read it to me on my wedding day and then had immediately taken the papers and locked them in his office (which I had to break into in order to get them back). I also realized that he would most likely not hold true to his words. So I made sure that my children and I had the basics we needed to leave.

I can remember the day I finally got the courage to tell Richard I had filed for divorce. I was nervous because I had no clue how he would react. I was scared that he would not just react with verbal abuse but also with physical abuse. I feared for my safety. I knew, however, there would never be a perfect moment to tell him, and I could not keep dragging the relationship out. For my sake and for my children's sake, I had to get it over with and speak up. We were upstairs in his house and had begun arguing once again about him cheating. Richard began to walk into the other room, and I took a chance and let the words fall from my mouth.

"Richard, I filed for divorce." As I spoke, my voice felt weak at first, but saying those words out loud for the first time gave me confidence. I had finally taken charge of my life and was finally learning how to stand up for myself. The moment I let the words out, Richard turned around in the doorway and stared me dead in the eyes. He had a look of shock on his face. I knew he did not believe me.

I began to slowly back up. He seemed unusually calm, but I didn't feel safe. Since the day I married him, I had never felt safe when he was drunk or angry, and that day he was both. He didn't break eye contact and continued to glare at me, taking a long moment before he replied. The silence between us was stiffening. I took another step back, and I could feel the edge of the first stare. I held onto the railing, and he suddenly took a step forward. I was scared out of my mind. With Richard, I was always guessing what would happen next. He was constantly finding new ways to remain in control.

His voice was low and his words were drawn out as he replied, "I will destroy you."

My hands gripped the railing tighter, and I continued to slowly walk back down the stairs. I was holding my cell phone in my hands, and Richard reached out to grab it from me. I quickly pulled away, retreated down the steps, and went outside to avoid any further argument.

After telling Richard I had filed for divorce, the tension in the house was very thick. He had always said that he would be the one to file for divorce first. Richard was not used to women standing up to him. I tried my best to avoid him. I never wanted a messy divorce, but he had other plans. I knew the chances of Richard kicking us out of his house were almost certain, so I tried my best to reason with him to give us some time while I found somewhere to go with the children.

My suspicions were correct. About two days later, on a gloomy Sunday evening, around six o'clock, as the rain was pouring down, a delivery man appeared at the door. I answered the doorbell and was given flowers. At first, I thought that it was an apology, but I was wrong. The flowers had a restraining order attached to the stems. I was being thrown out, along with the kids.

The restraining order said that I needed to leave within a few hours. Although I was not surprised, I was upset. There were no tears, though. He didn't deserve my time or energy, and I did not want Leonardo and Victoria to see me cry. I gathered up my clothes and what little else I could and told Leonardo to pack the things that were important to him. He nodded and did as he was told. But upon telling Victoria, she couldn't believe it. She was still very young and had grown attached to Richard, and she was devastated that he could do this to us.

During our four-year marriage, I feared that if I left Richard, Brian would use it as a reason to gain custody of the children. Richard knew that, so he used it against me. I also knew that if I left Richard, or if Richard kicked me out, the children would most likely have to leave their schools. Leaving home crushed Leonardo, since he loved the school he was attending. He was on the water polo and the football teams, and because he was committed to them, he refused to leave at first. Victoria was inconsolable that Richard could hurt us like this. She was so little when we got married that she thought of him as a substitute dad. It broke her heart to leave. I had tried to keep quiet about most of what I was going through because I was afraid to upset Richard, and I wanted to protect them from the ugliness of his behavior. Even though Sabella and Leonardo were old enough to suspect something was going on, for Victoria, the trauma of being thrown out was more abrupt.

So we quickly packed what things we could, and we left. Being forced to leave was probably one of the hardest things that I had to do as a mom. It meant my children and I were leaving financial security and a roof over our heads. It meant leaving our life as a family, no matter how abusive this one was for me. It also meant that we left all our possessions, including items that were special to me, like the children's baby pictures and the crafts and items my children had created and collected over the years. We left a lot of precious memories behind that day. With the time constraints we were given, we did not have the ability to take everything; we simply left with the small number of items that we needed to live on.

With the help of a good friend, we left within the allotted four-hour time period he had given us. Even though my friends helped us move out, everything happened so quickly that we could not take all our possessions with us. Leonardo had to leave his video games and train collection, which he had started building when he was three years old, and Victoria had to leave the trampoline she loved. She continued to talk about it for a long time after we left. She also had to leave her Barbie car that she loved to ride around outside, and many other toys that were special to her. Leaving our dog behind was the hardest on her. We had to leave the little dog behind because we didn't have a place to keep her, and then, once we found a place, Richard refused to give our belongings back, including the dog. Losing everything was devastating for the children. My heart was broken, and I could not gather the words to explain to them the mistake I had made marrying someone I barely knew. It was very difficult for them, because they were missing the home that they had grown to love. It took a lot of time and therapy for the children to overcome this loss.

Even though I had my car, I was afraid to park it where Richard could see it and find me. The car was the one Richard gave to me, but it was in his name, and I did not want him to take it back. I relied on the car to take the kids to and from school and to try to get jobs. I was in a constant state of stress, to the point that I was unable to sleep. I knew, however, that I had to learn to take everything one day at a time and to keep moving forward. After I met Richard, I went from standing on my own two feet to being dependent on him, and he took it all away because I didn't know how to protect myself legally from him.

In the end, we weren't homeless for long, because our friend allowed us to move in with her, which gave me time to search for a place of our own.

As soon as we got settled in, I knew I needed to reassure my kids we would be okay. I told Leonardo and Victoria that we would find a place in the same school district so they would not have to leave their friends and school. I also told them to concentrate on their studies, to get good grades, and not to let all of this bother them. I assured them that I was going to take care of everything. To inspire Leonardo, I made a big promise to him that when he graduated, I would have a limousine take him to the graduation ceremony. I prayed that I would be successful in fulfilling my dreams for them. However, I was secretly afraid I would not be able to, because of all the obstacles.

We had a place to stay, thanks to my friend, but we had lost nearly everything and would have to start over. My kids were worried that I could not find a place to live in that school district, since at that time I was not working, and the school they attended was in an upper-middle-class section of the city. To make sure I reached my goal as fast as possible, I had to come up with a plan yet again. Along with the anguish of all that had happened, I knew I had to quickly get a job and make money, find us a place of our own to live, keep my children in the same school, and consult a lawyer to help me in my divorce. So I did what I knew I could do and started up my cleaning business again. I reconnected with my old clients and kept the business small so I could make enough money but also have some time to start piecing my life back together. I also found a job bartending on the weekends.

Every morning I would wake early enough to drive them to school so they could continue their education in the same place. The counselors at the school talked to the children frequently and checked in on them often, which helped them a lot during this tough transition.

Continuing to pay the lawyer to help me was challenging. Richard had a lot of money and I did not; he had the ability to keep arguing while the fees added up. Thankfully, I was able to come up with the money in order to pay the lawyer. I fought hard to force Richard to follow the prenuptial agreement he had made me sign. After all, I had stayed home for a long time serving him.

After we were divorced, Richard refused to leave me alone, and he would randomly show up at my work. He also began to delay his alimony payments, which was difficult for me because I had to call him to ask for it. After some time, he stopped following the court order and stopped paying me each month. I no longer had the money to continue fighting him, and I had no desire to keep seeing him, so in the end he didn't pay me what he was supposed to. He still owes me money to this day.

It was extremely difficult to find a house on our budget, but we did. I found a small rental house that we could call home in the school district, so my children would not have to give up their friends and the activities they participated in. Little by little, we decorated the house and made it feel like a home. The children were excited to have their own rooms once again. Victoria was excited to decorate her room, and I took her shopping to get a few new things for her new space. She loved pink at the time, and we found white furniture and pink decorations. She had a bunch of stuffed animals, especially stuffed dogs, that she placed on her bed. I tried my best to make the children feel comfortable and happy in the house. After finding a house, I was still busy but decided to go back to school and take some general education classes so I could make long-term career plans.

Despite our circumstances, my son always watched out for his little sister and worked hard to achieve his goals. He finished high school with honors, and on time. He got a large scholarship to a private university, and I kept my promise of bringing him to his graduation in a white limousine, surrounded by friends and family. I even wore a little polka-dotted dress as a tribute to what I wore for the ceremony that helped me get Leonardo back so many years before.

What I tell myself and my kids is this: "Life is like a baseball game. You may not hit a home run every time you come up to bat, but if you keep your eye on the ball and stay focused on what you are trying to do, you are bound to hit a grand slam one day. You just can't give up."

Nuevo Comienzo (New Beginning)

However scary the experience of us leaving home and starting over was, I kept thinking of the expression, "When one door closes, another one opens." That is exactly what happened to me when I started up my cleaning company again. Through the same cleaning business that led me to Richard, I received a phone call from a doctor who saw my ad in the paper. The doctor wanted my crew to help clean her home, and though I didn't know it yet, she was going to help turn my life around.

I had wanted to go into the medical field since I had given birth to Leonardo, but I didn't have the time or the knowledge of how to do it. Everything had been so confusing for me at the time, especially because it was hard to understand exactly what was happening. Problems created by my lack understanding English were compounded because of the lack of interpreters available while I was in the hospital and the courtroom. My situation made me want to learn how to help others, possibly by translating for Hispanic people who needed it. Just like other people who could not speak the language in a frightening medical situation, I had cried those same tears. I had experienced the pain and frustration of learning a new language. And though it was difficult, I did make it through, and I knew that someday, with my interpreting abilities, I could help someone who needed it. By this point in my life, my English was much better.

After sending my cleaning crews to the doctor's house for a while, I decided that I would try to go to her home myself so I could make a good impression and possibly get some information about the medical field. Once I talked to her a little more, I finally decided to ask her about joining the medical field. She thought this was a great idea, and we went over colleges that I could go to and what I would need to learn before entering the field. She told me that it was going to be a lot of hard and meticulous work, but St. Louis needed people like me to help. When I told Sabella I was going to go to college, she was excited for me. Since she was in school to become a nurse, she was happy that I was joining the medical field, and it gave us more to talk about.

Per the doctor's advice, I volunteered at a clinic where she worked, and while I was there, I learned more about the needs of the Hispanic community. I worked with doctors there, and I also learned a lot about the medical field, which helped me to realize that I wanted to be a medical assistant.

While attending school to become a medical assistant, I met a wonderful teacher, who was also the director of the school. She taught me to start from basic knowledge and work up by breaking down the more complicated information into segments I could understand. I could not have done it without her.

Asking her for advice about life helped me as well. She told me, "Just to be part of the world takes a lot of effort, dedication, and the ability to know the difference between getting your world as perfect as you want and just letting your dream world pass you by." She added, "The world is a circle, and you are the only person who can get in and start turning your life in the right direction."

Her words motivated me. I had never heard anything so true, then or now. For me, it meant believing in one's self, which makes such a difference to each of us as individuals and, in turn, to the world.

Deciding to pursue my dreams was difficult but worth it. With two children, I had a full schedule. Sabella was away with her dad at the time. It was difficult not having Sabella around, but she decided to stay in Texas and go to college near where her dad was living. Even though we were both super busy with school, we still managed to talk nearly every day. I missed her very much, but I was proud that she was pursuing a college education. Leonardo and Victoria had school and activities that they participated in. I went to school full time, which kept me busy. I would record my classes so I could listen to them as I was completing everyday tasks, such as cooking dinner or driving in the car. I would use the time when my children were at their activities to complete my homework and study. It was difficult to do, but I found a way. While I was in school, I kept my cleaning business. Thankfully, I was able to hire someone to help me manage and run it, so I could focus on my studies during the week. On Saturdays, I worked at a bar to bring in extra money. I had previous experience in the industry, and I had found that working with people and communicating with customers improved my English, and it was fun. I met some very nice, as well as important, people through my work.

At school and on my job, I worked hard at doing my best. Because of my dedication and my grades, I was chosen to give a speech at graduation and was given a special cord of honor to wear with my cap and gown for having perfect attendance and excellent grades. The day of the ceremony, I was so happy to see my three children sitting in the audience smiling back at me while I was speaking. I am still in touch with many people that I met through college, and I can confidently say that I know more than I could have ever imagined because of these encouraging people.

When I finished college and received my certificate as a Registered Medical Assistant, I immediately went to work. Around this time, I decided to close my cleaning business so I could begin focusing on creating a solid, long-lasting career in the medical field. I started my internship working with the doctor who had first encouraged me to go to school, and I was pleasantly surprised when her office staff hired me full time a week later to fill the position of a medical assistant phlebotomist. It was an incredible experience. After working there for about three years, I noticed I would be able to help more people if I received the qualifications to be an interpreter.

So I took time off medical assisting and went back to school to become a medical and legal interpreter to help more people in the Hispanic community in the future. I wanted to become a voice for those who could not speak for themselves and help them to understand their legal or health situations. To enhance my skills, I also earned a certification for interpreting and cultural competency in mental health settings, which qualified me to work with people who have mental health issues. This helped me understand how to help myself, as well as others who battle with depression and anxiety. Learning more about mental health issues allowed me to realize I wasn't alone, and there are a lot of women (as well as men and children) who experience depression, anxiety, and sadness. Today, I enjoy my job as an interpreter, and I also spend a lot of time volunteering with the Hispanic community, especially by visiting safe places where women who have recently escaped abusive situations can go and seek refuge. I couldn't be happier with the decision I made to become an interpreter, because it has opened doorways for me to assist and encourage people who are going through situations that are very similar to the ones I have already overcome.

LOVE AND FAITH GO TOGETHER

After several years of being on my own, I was free from intimidating men. My life was my children and my job, and it felt good to be independent. After everything I had walked through, I never wanted to *have* to depend on a man again. I had worked very hard on my own to become stable and strong once again. I was doing well providing for myself and for my children, who were starting to get older. Since I was so busy, I didn't think I had time for a relationship. Despite my hectic schedule and all I had been through in the past in the name of love, I always kept up my hope and faith that I would find someone to truly trust and to share my life with, but I didn't worry about when that would happen. Most of all, that someone had to be a good person, someone who would be kind and honest, and this was worth waiting for, even if that meant a very long wait. I knew I never wanted to go back to being with someone who treated me badly. Unless he was a good person who knew love meant mutual respect and caring, I would not want to risk putting myself or my kids through another bad relationship. So I made sure I was able to take care of myself and was truly happy with where I was at in my life before I would reopen my heart to love.

Though meeting someone was not on my mind at the time, I had not given up on love. It took a few years before I was ready to think about letting someone into my life. Before I met my current husband—the person who would become the love of my life—I was just starting to think, "Maybe I won't get the chance to meet someone I can trust enough."

I was bartending when I met him. I noticed him the moment he walked in. He was well put together. His shirt was tucked in, his hair was combed nicely, and he looked very clean-cut. I thought he was handsome, to say the least, but shy, with an air of fractured confidence. It was not that he was unsure of himself, but it just seemed that he was a little hesitant and didn't know what he was supposed to say when he sat down at the bar.

When he came in, I was speaking to one of my favorite customers and her mother, but I paid attention when he stepped through the door—I had never seen him before. Considering that I had worked at this restaurant for a while, I usually knew everyone who walked in, either as a regular or a previous visitor, so this was an unusual occurrence. When I looked over at him, it was obvious he was watching me, and he smiled when he saw me looking his way.

My customer got a kick out of seeing this quiet gentleman and me glancing at each other from across the room, and after sizing up the situation, she encouraged me to talk to him.

It was a busy night, but I didn't want to waste any time. I told him hello and gave him some salsa, tortilla chips, and a glass of water, and then I continued making drinks for other customers and going about my business as usual. The bar had a mirror along the back, and as I glanced at it, his gaze was the same—he was still looking at me.

I worked quickly, making sure everyone was completely set on drinks and food so that I could have just a few minutes to talk to him. I walked back over and asked if he would like to try "my special margarita," with top-shelf tequila, triple sec, and fresh citrus. He agreed, and for the rest of the night, we chatted over the bar and between the waves of customers coming in.

"My name is Argentina. What's yours?" I asked at last.

"Hi there, Argentina. My name is David," he said with a smile.

As the night grew long, another regular came into the restaurant. Knowing that this was a bit of a favor, I pleaded with him to find out about this man that I had been talking to all night, and he agreed. Drink in hand, he strolled to the bar and chatted up the handsome gentleman that I had my eye on. He turned to me multiple times and winked, letting me know that I was all clear—he appeared to be a good guy.

Feeling reassured, I returned to the bar where my new acquaintance was sitting. We made eye contact a few times, and then it was time for him to go. He gave me his number, and he was on his way.

David interested me, and our connection, although brief, gave me hope for love. As the days went by, he came in time and time again, and though our conversations were short, for me they were thrilling. One Saturday, David came in and started up a conversation with me about his love for baseball, and my heart fluttered because I shared that love of baseball from my childhood in the Dominican Republic. As the conversation developed, he told me he was a season ticket holder, and then he offered me tickets to a Cardinals game. This was my chance, my 'ticket' to get to know him. He handed me the tickets, and I asked him to join my children and me. He said yes.

When we went to the game, I could tell immediately that David was a great guy. My children got along with him from the first time they met him. We had a lot of fun that day. After that game, David and I saw each other more and more frequently, and it didn't take long until he became part of my children's life. He invited my children and me to more baseball games, and we went out to eat together often. David had never had any children and enjoyed spending time with Leonardo and Victoria. When Sabella would come into town, we would have family barbeques. David loved my cooking and the Dominican dishes I made, which was a plus. David became very involved and would attend my children's school activities with me. I could tell he genuinely cared for my children, and I was happy to know that my three children liked David. To me, he was perfect: he was kind and considerate, and the brightness of his eyes lit up my soul. It was like David was handed to me at the perfect time, in the perfect place. I had never lost my faith that I would find someone who was a good person, and in my mind, he was my reward.

Although I had met David through my work as a bartender, one thing I found particularly worrisome after getting to know him was his alcohol dependency. When I realized he was an alcoholic, I told him I also struggled with alcoholism, but I was planning to quit drinking and that if he wanted a relationship with me, he would have to do the same. So I asked David to enter rehab and get clean.

Knowing that my father had passed away from drinking made me want to stop drinking. I knew I had been drinking too much, and working at the bar didn't help. After divorcing Richard, I had continued to drink. I knew that I should have gotten some help, but I was far too dependent on alcohol to give it up and drank in an attempt to feel happier. I knew I had to stop because I was now building my career as an interpreter, and the more I drank, instead of feeling happier, I became more depressed. The children and I were still doing fine, but I knew that it was time to quit drinking. I began to understand how important it was for us to get through it together. Working in the medical field and interpreting at the court taught me a lot about the dangers of alcohol. It persuaded me even more to quit drinking once and for all.

I started gathering information and learned about several free programs and resources that were available to me. I knew in my heart that if I wanted something done, I needed to do it myself. After hesitating for a while, I gained the courage to take a step in the right direction and began to move forward toward my goal of overcoming my struggles with alcohol. I discovered that there is a lot of free information available through libraries, churches, and websites, and also by simply reaching out to those I trusted. I first had to learn to not be embarrassed any longer by my struggles and admit that I had a problem, and then I was able to seek the help I needed.

David and I made it a point to go to Alcoholics Anonymous together. We both had fun making friends, and we supported each other's growth through these meetings. They are an amazing resource, and they are free of charge. What I learned is that you cannot force someone to change. If you expect a different person in a relationship, you may be disappointed. However, because we were both willing to make sacrifices for each other in our relationship, we worked to get past it. That was the key factor, I discovered. It was the willingness to make sacrifices and grow with each other, rather than expecting only the other person to change.

To me, David was a godsend. I talked to God on a daily basis (and still do) to keep my faith strong and my hopes high, and David was God's gift back to me. This gift of love and partnership wasn't handed to me, but it was presented as an opportunity to grow together.

Getting rid of alcohol in my life wasn't easy (especially while working as a bartender), but it was worth it. Once I quit drinking, I did lose one of my friends because of it. She didn't seem to enjoy my company as much as she had before, and eventually we drifted apart. It was sad, but I realized that she could not have been a true friend if she wanted me to continue to hurt myself with alcohol. Even though I miss her, I learned to love myself more, and I know I did the right thing. Even now, I still go out for drinks with my friends, mine being alcohol-free, of course. But it's still fun to be with them. I don't need substances to have fun, and that's okay—both for me and my friends. Now that I am no longer drinking, I feel like I have control over my life and have become healthier and happier.

STARTING AGAIN

As David and I continued to grow closer, I knew it was time to tell him about all the events, good and bad, that had brought me to this point. I told him everything, including about my father's anger, abuse, and alcoholism, about the poor choices I had made for the fathers of my wonderful children, and about how, because of the abuse, I had struggled with anxiety and depression off and on for most of my adult life but had not really talked about how I was feeling or understood what was going on with me. It was during this time, when Leonardo was about to leave for college, my depression got worse, and I started having nightmares about when he was stolen from me at the hospital. I was so afraid that I was going to lose him forever, since that was the first time he left my sight for more than just a couple of days.

I decided to go back to the mountain town where it all began and review the court records, to face my fears and get some closure. My good friend Lucecita graciously agreed to go with me to review the court papers that I did not understand so long ago. However, when I started to revisit the scene of so much pain, the awful memories haunted me. I began to have a panic attack. My blood pressure soared up and would not go down, and I began crying uncontrollably and freaked out. Lucecita took me to the hospital.

When I came to my senses again, I couldn't believe it; I was in a hospital back in the same town where I had lost my child so long ago. Although I didn't realize it at the time, I was suffering from severe depression. While I was there, I saw a psychiatrist who talked with me and told me that, in his opinion, I had been living with depression for a long time. My anxiety stemmed from my childhood growing up in an abusive household, and because I never got help for it, it continued to get worse as I went through my adult life. The addition of anxiety and sadness over my son going away to college finally climaxed to the point where it was far too much for me to handle. He gave me medication for my anxiety and said I needed to continue therapy when I returned home.

I returned home, and David saw me at my lowest point and stayed by my side during this rough time. He earned my trust, and I knew I could tell him what happened. I had held everything inside for so long, and I could not handle staying silent any longer. We continued to talk openly about everything, and I realized he wasn't going anywhere. He loved me, and I loved him, and as I was working through my pain, he was always there and understood. I began to see a psychiatrist and was diagnosed with depression, as well as anxiety. I took my medicine and started to feel better, but I found if I didn't take my medicine or bottled up sad feelings, the anxiety would start up, and then the feelings of depression would follow. I learned that anxiety exhibits through intense worry, fear, flashbacks of past painful experiences, the inability to sleep, and having jumpy and jittery feelings, which can all lead to feeling down, and if the down feelings go on too long, they can lead to depression.

While trying to recover, I would walk, listen to music, and do everything I could think of to stay busy. I knew that the medicine alone would not save me, but I had to choose to do tasks that brought me joy and stay away from the dark gloominess that can easily fall over a person who does not stay focused on what is ahead. I became disciplined about the counseling and the meds. At first, I saw the psychiatrist once a week, and as I improved, it was only every other week, and then it was only when I needed to check in. I learned that when I started to feel sad, I could not ignore my feelings anymore. I talked to my psychiatrist, a friend, or my pastor. Being diagnosed with depression also helped me to understand the patients I worked with better. I could relate to the things they were going through and feeling.

Through this difficult time, David continued to stay by my side and was there for me and for my children. I knew I had finally found someone that respected me and would truly treat me and my kids well. One day, David took me to a park we would often visit to take walks, and he surprised me by asking me to marry him. I was overjoyed and said yes! We got married about a year after he proposed.

Shortly after we got engaged, Richard found out. He had continued to give me a hard time years after we divorced. One day, David was served with a long letter from Richard. The letter stated that I was a terrible person, wife, and mother and said I was garbage. It was an extremely brutal and nasty letter, and upon finding out, I was completely mortified. I had already opened up to David about my past and the bad choices I had made, including everything Richard had put me through, but I was still scared David would think of me differently after reading the letter. Thankfully, I had found a wonderful man who did not second-guess a single thing. He told me that Richard was in the past and not to worry about him any longer. We both agreed to put the letter behind us and move on.

David helped me to realize that I could move forward. I had spent so many years trying to fix my faults, but I realized that I needed to stop dwelling on the past. I knew that if I spent my life thinking about my past mistakes, I would miss enjoying the present and the future. I was in a new place in my life, and I began to see how far I had come. I loved that I had finally found someone who understood me; we truly brought out the best in each other.

On our wedding day, there I was at last, with the love of my life. I was in my beautiful dress chosen by my two lovely daughters, Victoria and Sabella; escorted by my wonderful and handsome son, Leonardo; surrounded by pink, white, red, and purple flowers in the Jewel Box in Forest Park in St. Louis. It was spring, and the weather was gorgeous. I felt so beautiful in my wedding dress, and I was so excited to wear it because this was my first time getting to wear a traditional wedding dress. For the first time in my life, I felt like I was my own person. I had come so far and was so much stronger. I had graduated college, had a stable job that I loved, and for the first time in a long time, I felt genuinely confident. I was getting married, on my terms, to a man I truly loved and respected, and by a pastor of my choosing, also for the first time. It was finally the way it should be, and I couldn't believe it was finally happening to me, in the right way, at last! I found that David added to my success and happiness—he completed me. I finally had a husband who was loved by my family. One of his sisters said I saved him, but I say we saved each other. It meant so much that both our families gave us their blessing.

Everything was just the way I imagined it would be. My friends and family were there, and the whole day was beautiful. I wanted to give David something from my heart, so I surprised him by writing him a song and sang it to him while we danced at the reception. The waters from the fountain in front of the building danced like we did all through the night. I can't help but think my wonderful grandmother, Rhafaela, was smiling down on me, knowing that I had found a love to last, but first I had found me. Now I was my own person and had set my secrets free.

Epilogue

Today, I am a medical and legal interpreter, which is my passion. Through my job, I help others who struggle not only with the language, but also with speaking up for themselves. When I sat down to write what had happened to me, it was hard, because I had never opened up about the pain I had gone through. I kept writing because I needed an outlet and a way to express myself. I also needed to tell my story. I had been quiet for so long, keeping the pain I had experienced locked in my heart, but I needed to let it out if I was ever to heal. At first I was afraid to tell my story, but I realized not having a voice was worse, and when I started talking and putting my thoughts into words, I felt better. I carried this weight around for so many years, and it was time to let it go. I was concerned at first by how others would look at me after hearing my story, but I knew the first step to overcoming was sharing what I had been through. Writing helped me to realize if I ever wanted to move forward, I had to stop blaming others and myself for everything in my past. I cannot begin to understand why bad things happen to us, but I do know that we must take the time to forgive others who hurt us and forgive ourselves for the decisions we've made. Most of all, I wanted Leonardo to know the truth; he deserved to know. Fighting for him with my entire heart, and not allowing obstacles to hinder my dreams, gave me strength, and this helped change the course of our family's journey.

During the difficult times, I discovered numerous programs and organizations that give both guidance and support. I learned that the first step is to ask for help. No matter how big or small the question or need is, you should never be embarrassed to ask. One organization I found through the internet is Celebrate Recovery, an incredible program that helped me learn how to cope and overcome the grief and hurt of my past. There are meetings held throughout the United States, and they are available free of charge. The program teaches people to overcome many different struggles, and the meetings are led by loving people who will listen. To overcome my alcohol addiction, I attended Alcoholics Anonymous meetings, which are also free of charge. While I was learning to control myself, it benefited me to attend these meetings. These organizations are meant to assist, but ultimately it is up to you to make a change, and the first step is seeking help.

Without these incredible, free resources, I would not be where I am today. I later discovered a few resources that I wish I had known about earlier in my life, when I was stuck in abuse and depression. The National Domestic Violence Hotline is available and can be called 24/7. Even if you do not speak English well, do not hesitate to call. They will find a way to help you and get you an interpreter.

Sometimes in distressing situations, it can feel as if you are boxed in with no hope of escape. For some of us, this can lead to anxiety and depression. Depression is one of the most painful feelings you can experience. It is a deep inner pain that is nearly impossible to comprehend or explain. When I was walking through depression, it was difficult for me to find the courage to seek help. I did not want to admit that I was hurting, and I feared what others would think of me. I did not want to be looked at differently or thought of as broken. Negative thoughts clouded my brain, and no matter how hard I tried, I could not push them from my heart or my mind. These thoughts controlled me. I felt completely trapped and like I was no longer in control of my life. When you are feeling depressed, it is important to tell someone how you are feeling. Talk to a family member, a friend, a counselor, or a doctor. Even if you feel like there is no one you can trust to tell, there is still hope. Behavioral Health Response is a helpful resource for those who are struggling with depression or going through a mental health crisis. They have trained counselors available 24/7 for anyone to call and talk to free of charge.

Celebrate Recovery: www.celebraterecovery.com
Alcoholics Anonymous: www.aa.org
National Domestic Violence Hotline: 1-800-799-7233
Behavioral Health Response: 1-800-811-4760
Suicide Prevention Lifeline: 1-800-273-8255

Lifeline Para la Prevención del Suicidio: 1-888-628-9454
Safe Connections (24/7 women's crisis hotline in St. Louis):
1-314-531-2003
Life Crisis Services (suicide prevention hotline):
1-314-647-4357

While I was in an abusive relationship, I never knew when my phone would be taken from me, so I wrote down important numbers on paper as backups to the ones I kept in my phone. It is important to have numbers somewhere that are easily accessible. Based on my experience and what I have observed through work, I advise the following: Always be aware of your surroundings and know where you are, in case of an emergency. In abusive relationships, it can be dangerous to fight back. I found that if I argued, then my abuser's anger intensified, and so did my chances of being hurt or harmed. I learned to listen and think through what I would say before responding. I discovered that what worked best for me was to think through decisions first, make a plan, and then try to find the safest way and the perfect moment to break free from my situation.

For years I bottled up my helplessness, which led to sadness and depression. When depressed, it can become easy to want to seclude oneself, but it is crucial to find someone to trust and to confide in. I am so grateful for my family and friends who were always there to listen, and to the programs, organizations, and my church that helped me along the way and inspired me to keep going.

Alongside feeling isolated, it was also difficult to find the desire to complete everyday tasks. I had to find a way to motivate myself. I had to find something, anything, that would inspire me to want to make it through another day. I suggest writing down goals, hopes, and dreams, and no matter how weak you may feel, keep pressing forward. For me, writing down things I wanted to accomplish gave me a reason to want to get up in the morning and start my day. Working out, going for walks, and going to the library can be good outlets for overcoming anxiety and depression. Find activities that get you out of the house and around others. It is important to find at least one good friend or family member to tell that you are being treated by a doctor.

If you take medication, it is very important to keep taking it. When I went without my medicine, it became easy to slide back into depression. Follow and trust what the doctors tell you, because they have gone through years of education, and they know what they are talking about. It can sometimes feel embarrassing to acknowledge a medical condition. It was difficult for me to admit that I was seeing a psychiatrist or taking medication, but I realized it is nothing to be ashamed of. Taking daily medication for depression or anxiety is no different than taking a daily medication for any other health condition, such as diabetes, high blood pressure, and many others; it is nothing to be ashamed of.

Prayer also helped me to get through every difficult situation I came face to face with. For me, it was important to keep my faith strong and steadfast. My faith is something that I have had my whole life, but it is something I have struggled with sometimes. I prayed every day, even when I thought that with all that was going on in the world, God did not have time for me. I never fully understood why bad things happened to me or to anyone, but I knew that God was always there to listen. And because of that, I felt calm and comfortable each time I prayed. I had faith that I would always make it through as long as I set goals for myself and did not allow myself to waver in seeing them accomplished. When I prayed, I would try to focus on thanking God for the good things He had given me. It is easier to fail while concentrating on the bad. By shifting my focus to the good things, I was given an extra amount of confidence that God was in control from start to finish.

Regardless of what was going on in my life, I made sure to concentrate on the good and tried to focus on how far I had come. I also began volunteering, and it made me feel like I had a purpose in life. Helping others helped me to feel like I had something to give. Dedicating time to help others can help shift your perspective on life and can be a good way to keep motivated. Volunteering gave me something to be passionate about and pour my heart into. There are many places available to volunteer, such as nursing homes, houses for abused women, and children's homes.

Anxiety and depression can be an issue for people who are isolated by language, poverty, or trauma. Some adults are embarrassed or afraid to admit they are having emotional problems or don't know how to get help. Teens and children can be affected too, and they often don't even tell their parents they are depressed. They can start with a school counselor, who can also put them in touch with resources available in the community.

Even though, for some of us, getting an education seems nearly impossible, it is essential to move forward. Whether it is achieving an associate's degree or going to trade school, it could mean the difference in ensuring a solid career. As a woman, it can be difficult to find time to go to school while taking care of children and working a job, but it is crucial to find a way. It may mean a few years of chaos and tough obstacles, but it will be worth it. In my case, I knew I had to go to school and start a career if I ever wanted to be independent and be able to provide my children with the life they deserved and give them their best shot at life.

Today, I have finished school, have a degree, and have taught my children the importance of education. Sabella has gone through nursing school and has a bachelor's degree in nursing and is now a registered nurse, Leonardo graduated from a private university with a bachelor's degree in criminal justice and now works in the field, and Victoria has just started taking college classes.

When I look back today, the most important lesson I have learned in my life is believing in myself. It took a long time to realize, but learning to believe in myself was the key to my success. Anything is possible, but it is up to each of us to make it happen. We are stronger than we think. Being fearless, courageous, and bold will help us overcome any obstacle that comes our way. I sincerely hope that anyone in a situation of abuse, physically, mentally, or emotionally, like I was, will find the strength to get out.

For anyone struggling in this situation, I share your pain. Know that you are not alone, and there are so many like you in the world. Once you find someone who will listen, or an organization where you can get help, do not be timid and do not remain quiet—you are the only one who can take the first step. Remember, silence is not an option. Speaking up can be your bridge to freedom.

It is my great joy that my children are doing well and are growing up—or have grown up—to be loving, caring people. While the path may not have been easy, they have always known that they were loved by me and by their extended family. It is important to me that they have read my story and have offered their support for me to finish it. Leonardo and Sabella, who are grown now, both wanted to contribute their comments from their perspective. (Additionally, Leonardo shot and contributed the photograph used on the cover of this book, which I am thankful for.) Victoria, my youngest, who has no problem speaking up for herself, may never have to experience the issues I did from not revealing my truth. Even though she said she was not comfortable discussing her perspective for the book at this time, she is okay being included in the book.

NOTE FROM LEONARDO

My earliest memory is of me sitting on a very comfy, child-sized lounge chair. I was probably about three years old, and I was watching while my mom vacuumed around me, pretending the vacuum was a monster, and I'd just jump back onto my lounge chair. We would have a nice laugh together. She would walk away and then sneak up on me again, and she would do this continuously until she was done with vacuuming.

Although her work schedule was tricky, we somehow managed to have dinner together as a family almost every night. We'd all sit on the sofa together in the living room watching reruns of *Full House.* Even when we were struggling, my mom seemed to hold our family together. She is one of the nicest people I know. She could also be very serious when she had to be. If I did something wrong, she would sit me down, or chase after me if she had to. She would teach me the lesson, and then she made sure I never did it again.

I remember when I was a little brat, around five or six, I stole some money from my mom's purse because I wanted to take it to school and show it off to my fellow classmates. Later that day, my mom showed up at my school when she discovered the money was missing. She asked if I knew where her money went. I played dumb and told her I had no idea! Later, I realized, "How am I going to get this money back to her purse without her noticing?"

When she picked me up, she was waiting with a grin on her face, wanting to see my backpack. That's when I knew I was in trouble. After she found the money, she sat me down and talked to me for what seemed like an hour, teaching me lessons: about money and stealing and gratefulness, and the most important one of all: forgiveness. She forgave me for stealing 100 dollars that were supposed to go to bills that I'm sure were due at the time. That blew my mind. Unfortunately, that didn't get me out of being grounded for a while.

I remember being nine years old or so, and my mom would take me and my little sister to school with her a couple times a week so we could spend time together. She would drop us off at the college's day care while she would go to her English class for the night. On the drive home, we would sit in the car and sing along to whatever CD we had decided to play. The music my mom selected would always be uplifting. There were some days she would tear up during the song and just look at me and my sister and say, "I love you."

When I was around 11 years old, my mom started her own house cleaning business and asked me to create a name. To me, it was so cool that she entrusted me with this important task. I took this very seriously and made a huge list of names until had I picked the perfect name. That same year, my mom decided it was about time we all got baptized. I was excited about this; my sister and I enjoyed going to church on Sundays, mostly for the music and the chance of convincing our mom to stop at IHOP on the way home.

I have now graduated from a university and have started working. I have many friends and couldn't ask for anything better. I am very healthy, and my mom makes sure of that. After I read this book, I feel even more proud of my mom and everything that she has done for my siblings and me. She is one of the strongest women I know. I love her and know that I would not be where I am today without my mom's perseverance to fight for us and to be the best mom ever.

Note from Sabella

Strong, smart, and loving—these are only a few words that come to my mind when I think of my mother. My mother is strong because the journey she has traveled has not been exactly a fairy tale of unicorns and rainbows. Can you imagine having to fight for your child in fear of losing him forever? My mother, being of Hispanic descent, barely knowing any English, having no money, a lapsed visa while waiting for it to renew, and no family near for thousands of miles, had to face a judge and convince her that she was indeed worthy of keeping her child. At that time, I have no doubt she felt hopeless, alone, and betrayed, but she remained strong because she wanted her children to be strong. And we are.

My mother is also smart, as evidenced by all her accomplishments. My mother, a young, kind-hearted girl with a humble background, managed to become a U.S. citizen, went to school, and eventually became an independent business owner. There are so many other paths she could have taken, other decisions she could have made, but she made smart ones because she wanted her kids to be smart. And we are.

My mom always tried to create memories that we would remember forever. I can remember countless exciting adventures we shared. She is finally happy alongside a wonderful man who loves her and appreciates her, protects her, and even spoils her. My mother is loving; her love is like no other. Even though she and I have not always been together, she has been one of the only constants in my life. I have always known that her sweet voice of kindness and great advice is only one phone call away. She has always taught us to be kind and to never repay evil with evil but with forgiveness and love, because she wanted her kids to be loving. And we are. Thank you, mom, for being strong, smart, and loving, because these are values that will be passed on to your future generation.

Victoria

When my youngest child, Victoria, was growing up, we had a very close relationship and a special bond, maybe because she was the baby of the family. We would do a lot of things together, like going bike riding, getting our nails done, and going shopping. I valued her opinion and wanted her to be happy above all else. She was my only child still living at home, because Sabella was back in Texas and Leonardo was college-bound. I wanted to make sure Victoria truly liked David, and she was very open about how she felt toward him. She was getting older and was able to form her own opinions. I have always been proud of the fact that she is able to speak her mind and unafraid to say what she feels.

Victoria is now a full-time student and also works full time as a banker. She still lives at home with David and me. She has always been mature for her age, and a responsible person. When she was in high school, she kept busy and was very dedicated to several extracurricular activities. I loved attending her school choir performances and cheering her on at cross-country meets and swim meets.

She has many friends that she hangs out with regularly. She loves working out and playing with her dog, Honey. I could not be happier that she still lives with me, and I get to see her daily. Currently, she tells me is not ready to share her feelings and relive the story, and I respect that and her for speaking her mind.

ACKNOWLEDGMENTS

Along my journey of sharing my story, I have been blessed with numerous people who have both motivated and encouraged me. Without the friends, family, and mentors who were always there for me, it would have been very difficult to finish this book.

I would like to thank my editor, Andrew Doty, for helping me to connect all the dots and for bringing my book to life. I would also like to thank Susan Fechter for coaching me and guiding me through the writing process. I appreciate you taking the time to have tea with me and discuss my story. Thank you for answering when I called and for giving me honest and well-thought-out feedback. You helped me to breathe new life into my story, draw my voice out from within myself, and help this book along its path to where it is now. I am very grateful for you. Thank you to my friend Emma Norman for the time spent reading and helping me with my book. I appreciate you very much. Thank you, Kari Melendez, Charles Newton, Mr. Barklage, and Pastor JT for reading my book and giving me your feedback.

I would like to thank Dr. Rosa Myles for encouraging me to join the medical field and inspiring me to go back to college. You helped me to see that I could indeed take control of my life and go as far as my dreams would take me. I would like to thank my friend Brandy Scheer and her family for allowing my children and me to stay with them until we found our own place.

To my family, I am glad we have always found a way to stay close even though we live miles apart. Most importantly, I would like to thank my wonderful husband for loving me exactly the way that I am, and for understanding that my past is part of my future. For my children, who light up my life with joy, I thank God each day.

ABOUT THE AUTHOR

Argentina Parra grew up in the Dominican Republic and moved to the United States in her early twenties. Shortly after moving to America, her dream took a wrong turn. Despite the fact that she walked through many years of physical, mental, and emotional abuse, she has continued to persevere and overcome each trial she has faced with strength. *Silence Is Not an Option* is the inspiring, emotional, and courageous memoir of how she managed to stand up for herself against anxiety, depression, and abusive relationships.

Today, Argentina is a medical and legal interpreter with a medical assistant associate's degree and currently works in St. Louis with the Hispanic community. She is happy that she can be a bridge to help, guiding people through intense difficulties. Argentina is happy with where her life has brought her, and her desire is to help others discover how to find beauty in the ashes and to grow and blossom in the midst of pain.

To learn more about the author or to contact her, visit ArgentinaParra.com.

CPSIA information can be obtained
at www.ICGtesting.com
Printed in the USA
FFHW021649140119
50171784-55103FF